I0140531

America's Wake Up Call

America's Wake Up Call

FREEDOM FROM RELIGIOUS BONDAGE

❦

Chris Leffler

Copyright © 2016 Chris Leffler
All rights reserved.

ISBN: 0990624447
ISBN 13: 9780990624448

I have chosen not to capitalize the name satan because he doesn't deserve it nor is he worthy of it.

All Scripture quotations are taken from King James Version of the Bible

Cover design by Ben Hawkes, www.hawkeseyedesign.com.

Acknowledgements

I WOULD LIKE TO THANK my wife Susan for helping me with this book. A special thanks to Holy Spirit for giving me revelation and understanding of His word and for inspiring me to write this book. There is so much more for You to reveal to us in the knowledge of You and Your word and what you have planned for each and every one of us, that our minds can't comprehend, but I look forward to the journey and the mysteries that will unfold.

Table of Contents

Acknowledgements · vii

Chapter 1 What's This All About? · 1
Chapter 2 Who Do You Say That I Am? · · · · · · · · · · · · · · 19
Chapter 3 Rock Solid Foundation · · · · · · · · · · · · · · · · · · · 33
Chapter 4 The Goodness of God · · · · · · · · · · · · · · · · · · · 47
Chapter 5 Grace and Faith · 61
Chapter 6 Heal the Sick · 75
Chapter 7 Our Crumbling and Declining Nation · · · · · · · · 99

CHAPTER 1

What's This
All About?

❧

T<small>ODAY MOST OF THESE</small> so called spirit filled churches have fallen way short when it comes to teaching us just how much potential we have in Christ Jesus. My goal here is to teach us who we are in Christ as individuals, who are able to operate in both the power and authority that has already been made available to us as an inheritance.

Could it be that the church has gotten off track and we are no longer standing on the same foundation? It's the people who are born again believers in Christ that Jesus refers to as the church. Not some building or a separate group of people. Have we segregated ourselves into a bunch of different isolated groups? Could it be that even as we come together as a group many people have formed their own theological opinion, and are actually praying against each other?

The answer to this is yes. When some people are praying Old Testament prayers and begging or asking God to do something that Jesus has already provided for us as a finished work of the cross, it is releasing an atmosphere of unbelief. Praying Old Testament prayers has the potential to hinder the prayers of the New Testament believer. (We will go into much more detail about this later).

When we become more knowledgeable in knowing who we are in Christ, then we will be able to make a difference. When we come together as a corporate group praying and worshipping, we should become like an orchestra, each person being unique and having a very important part to play, yet still playing the same song. In other words, each person is operating in their gifting but all standing on the same theological foundation.

Is it possible that the modern day church has become so watered down and powerless that it lost its voice and influence on society? Is a lack of church influence resulting in a declining or failing governmental system? After all, according to the church we certainly would not want to offend anyone! Perhaps we should look at how Jesus dealt with people. He had a very important message to get across to us and He couldn't be concerned with whether or not He offended anybody.

This attitude about having to be so politically correct towards everyone is crippling the church today. We need to use some common sense of course when we minister to people, but not to the point of compromising what the word of God says. If we are going to get back on track then we need to rely on what the Bible says and start using it for what it was created for. It is our instruction manual on how to live life from God's perspective.

There really is no end to learning what the word of God has for us, it's a lifelong process of renewing our minds from a carnal way of thinking which is what the Bible calls walking after the flesh.

In order for us to walk after the spirit and not after the flesh, we must be transformed in our minds through the continual reading and listening to the Word of God.

However, we must be careful not to believe everything we hear, even when it comes from the pastor of a church, media, ministry, or other Christians who mean well and think they know more than they really do. We must also be careful about what we read. There are a lot of Christian books and teachings that can lead us in the wrong direction. Always take these things that you either hear or read and compare them to what the Bible says. If what you hear or read does not line up with scripture, then don't have anything to do with it.

The Bible warns us that there will be false prophets. A lot of what's being preached today does not line up with scripture. My theology is let God be true, but every man a liar who's word does not line up with scripture. *(Romans 3:4)*

Colossians 2:8 Beware lest any man spoil you through philosophy and vain deceit, after the traditions of men, after the rudiments of the world, and not after Christ.

Mark 7:13 Making the word of God of none effect through your tradition, which ye have delivered: and many such like things do ye.

We need to know the word so well that we meditate on it day and night, and then we will have good success. *(Joshua 1: 8)*

2 Timothy 3:16-17 All scripture is given by inspiration of God, and is profitable for doctrine, for reproof, for correction, for instruction in righteousness: That the man of God may be perfect, thoroughly furnished unto all good works.

2 Peter 1:20-21 Knowing this first, that no prophecy of the scripture is of any private interpretation. For the prophecy came not in old time by the will of man: but holy men of God spake as they were moved by the Holy Ghost.

According to these scriptures we know that the Bible was written by men who were under the inspiration of the Holy Spirit. Therefore, it was never meant for us to read with just head knowledge, and to analyze through just our carnal senses.

Although, if you are not familiar with the Bible you must read the word enough to know what the Bible is about in order for the Holy Spirit to be able to help you with renewing your mind so that you can learn scripture from a spiritual perspective. *(Romans 12:2)*.

Jesus explains that reading the word is like a farmer who plants seed in the ground: It has to sink down in the soil before it can begin to take root. He also describes our heart as being the soil were the seed (word) is planted.

Jesus gives us some examples of the conditions of the heart that can slow down or stunt the growth of the seed. He says in a parable that some of the seed fell by the way side, and the fowls of the air came and devoured it. And some fell on stony ground, but it had no root so when the sun came up it withered away. And some fell among thorns and the thorns choked it, and it yielded no fruit. And others fell on good ground and brought forth fruit, some a hundredfold, some sixtyfold, some thirtyfold.

His disciples asked Him what this parable meant and Jesus said the seed is the Word of God. Those by the way side are they that hear the word; then the devil comes and takes away the word out of their hearts. They that are on rocky ground are they, which, when they hear the word receive it with joy; until a time of temptation comes and then they fall away forgetting what they have learned. The ones that received seed among the thorns are those that hear the word; but the cares of this world, and the deceitfulness of riches, choke the word and they become unfruitful, because their focus is no longer on the word. But he that receives the seed into good ground is he that hears the word and understands it; they are the ones who bring forth fruit some a hundredfold, some, sixty, some thirty.

I like that Jesus gives us fruit as an example so we can visualize planting a seed in the ground. When we plant in good rich soil in a safe place, we can be confident that it will grow and produce fruit. It is the same thing with the word. As long as we keep our attention on what the Word of God says we will see results.

Try closing your eyes and seeing this in your mind; let your imagination paint a picture of the word as a seed going down and taking root. Think about this seed working and growing in you.

This picture of planting seeds is one of the first visions that I ever had. This has been an important process for me to learn how the word works towards renewing the mind because the best way to plant seed is to read the word for yourself. I know that this works because I had another vision later on of the word exploding inside me, as if I had eaten little capsules of faith filled words.

The Word of God is different. It's not like reading something out of other books. It is the spoken Word of God, the Word is alive! The Bible tells us that God spoke everything into existence: His word is alive and it will produce a positive change in us if we will just trust in Him, be patient and let that seed grow.

For more information about the parable of the seed and the sower, read Matthew chapter 13, Mark chapter 4, and Luke chapter 8. We learn by hearing and reading.

Romans 10:17 So then faith cometh by hearing, and hearing by the word of God.

John 6:63 It is the spirit that quickeneth; the flesh profiteth nothing: the words that I speak unto you, they are spirit, and they are life.

GOD'S GREATEST GIFT

The word quickeneth means to make alive. If we really want to understand in depth what the Bible is teaching us then we need to be able to follow the leading of the Holy Spirit. We need to allow Him to teach us and guide us in understanding the true meaning of scripture. We need the baptism of the Holy Spirit. I'm not talking about a water baptism, although that's important too, this baptism of the Holy Spirit is the promise that Jesus said he would send to us from God the Father *(Acts 1:4-5).*

However, the first thing you must do is to receive Jesus as your Lord and Savior. It is the Holy Spirit who first draws us to Jesus so we can be saved.

1 Corinthians 12:3…that no man can say that Jesus is the Lord, but by the Holy Ghost.

What Jesus does is come into your spirit, wipes away all your sins and creates in you a new, sanctified spirit. The Holy Spirit can only dwell in a spirit that is first made holy and righteous by Jesus. All you need to do is pray what is promised in Romans 10:9.

1 Corinthians 6:11 …but ye are washed, but ye are sanctified, but ye are justified in the name of the Lord Jesus, and by the Spirit of our God.

Romans 10:13 for whosoever shall call upon the name of the Lord shall be saved.

Romans 10:9 That if thou shall confess with thy mouth the Lord Jesus, and shall believe in thine heart that God has raised him from the dead, thou shalt be saved.

ACCEPTING JESUS AS YOUR LORD AND SAVIOR

This is between you and Jesus! You can say this prayer at home by yourself, or you can have someone assist you. Just say out loud:

Jesus I confess that you are my Lord and Savior. I believe in my heart that you died for my sins and that God raised you from the dead. By faith in your Word I now receive your free gift of salvation. Thank you Jesus for saving me.

Ephesians 2:8 For by grace are ye saved through faith; and not of yourselves: it is the gift of God.

It doesn't matter if you felt something or not. We receive Gods gifts through Jesus by faith. The gift of salvation is everlasting. Sin does not cause us to lose our salvation. Jesus paid for all of our sin, past present and future.

Romans 4:7-8 Saying, Blessed are they whose iniquities are forgiven, and whose sins are covered. Blessed is the man to whom the Lord will not impute sin.

Hebrews 10:12 But this man, after he had offered one sacrifice for sins forever, sat down on the right hand of God.

So what actually happened when you received Jesus as Lord?

2 Corinthians 5:17 Therefore if any man be in Christ, he is a new creature: old things are passed away; behold, all things are become new.

Most people really don't understand what this means, yet this is one of the most important keys to knowing who you are in Christ. Your physical body is not where this change took place. It's only in your spirit. You still look the same in your physical body. If you were to stand in front of a mirror and look yourself in the eye, you would not be able to see that anything changed. Neither did anything change in your soul. Your soul realm is your mind, will and emotions. It's your spirit that was changed when you received Jesus. Your spirit is the core of your being, it is the innermost part of you and it is what the Bible refers to as the heart of a man.

This can be somewhat confusing, because the Bible talks about the heart as being the inner man, and is referring to both the spirit and soul.

However, it is in your soul realm where the seed (God's Word) is planted. The soul realm is the place where our thoughts are conceived, the way we think will affect the things we say and that will directly determine what sort of result you will experience.

When you truly believe something, that's what is referred to as believing with your heart. And if you will stand firm and hold on to what is true, then you will begin to start seeing the manifestation of whatever that thought was. So if you are thinking about something bad, then your heart being good soil will start to grow that seed. This is why it is so important for us to renew our minds to what the Word of God says.

Renewing our minds through reading the Bible will cause our minds, which is our soul, to come into agreement with who we are in the spirit! This is how we release all of the benefits that are already in our born again spirit.

Proverbs 4:20-23 My son, attend to my words; incline thine ear unto my sayings. Let them not depart from thine eyes; keep them in the midst of thine heart. For they are life unto those that find them, and health to all their flesh. Keep thy heart with all diligence; for out of it are the issues of life.

There are two Hebrew words in the old testament that define the term heart: Leb and Lebab. Both of these words are similar in meaning and rarely refer to "heart" as the physical organ of the body, but rather they refer to the inner person. The New Testament uses the Greek word Kardia to define the term heart. Kardia is equivalent to the Hebrew terms leb and lebab and also refers to the heart as the center of the human but does not refer at all to the heart as a physical organ.

Proverbs 23:7 For as he thinketh in his heart, so is he…

Romans 8:27 And he that searcheth the hearts knoweth what is the mind of the Spirit, because he maketh intercession for the saints according to the will of God.

1 Corinthians 2:9-10 But as it is written, Eye hath not seen, nor ear heard, neither have enter in to the heart of man, the things which God hath prepared for them that love him. But God hath revealed them unto us by his Spirit: for the Spirit searcheth all things, yea, the deep things of God.

It is extremely important for us to understand just exactly what took place when we were born again in order for us to know who we are in Christ. Many Christians have been told that when you receive Jesus you also received the baptism of the Holy Spirit; this is not what the Bible teaches us. When you received Jesus, you received His Spirit. He exchanges your old sin nature spirit for His Spirit which is completely pure, righteous and holy. Your old sin nature spirit is completely gone, it can never come back again and is not something you still have that rises up again! IT IS GONE!

Ephesians 1:13-14 says that your new born again spirit was sealed with the Holy Spirit of promise until the redemption of the purchased possession. Nothing bad can ever enter into your born again spirit. The Holy Spirit of God is the only other Spirit that can ever enter into your born again spirit. Again, this is confirmed and backed up by scripture.

2 Corinthians 1:21-22 Now he which stablisheth us with you in Christ, and hast anointed us, is God; Who hath also sealed us, and given the earnest of the Spirit in our hearts.

Ephesians 4:30 And grieve not the holy Spirit of God, whereby ye are sealed unto the day of redemption.

Romans 6:6 Knowing this, that our old man is crucified with him, that the body of sin might be destroyed, that henceforth we should not serve sin.

Ephesians 4:22-24 That ye put off concerning the former conversation the old man, which is corrupt according to the deceitful lusts; And be renewed in the spirit of your mind; And that ye put on the new man, which after God is created in righteousness and true holiness.

Colossians 3: 9-10 Lie not one to another, seeing that ye have put off the old man with his deeds; And have put on the new man, which is renewed in knowledge after the image of him that created him.

Considering that Jesus and God the Father are one, when we received the Spirit of Jesus into our Spirit we also received the Spirit of God the Father: which is the Holy Spirit. They are three in one, Father, Son, and Holy Spirit.

John 10:30 I and my Father are one.

However this is not the baptism of the Holy Spirit that Jesus said He baptizes with. Let's look at some scriptures where Jesus talks about the Holy Spirit with His disciples.

John 14:26 But the Comforter, which is the Holy Ghost, whom the Father will send in my name, he shall teach you all things, and bring all things to your remembrance, whatsoever I have said unto you.

John 16:7 Nevertheless I tell you the truth; It is expedient for you that I go away: for if I go not away, the Comforter will not come unto you; but if I depart, I will send Him unto you.

John 14:16-17 And I will pray the Father, and he shall give you another Comforter, that he may abide with you forever; Even the Spirit of truth; whom the world cannot receive, because it seeth him not, neither knoweth him: but ye know him; for he dwelleth with you, and shall be in you.

John 20:21-22 Then said Jesus to them again, Peace be unto you: as my Father has sent me, even so send I you. And when he had said this, he breathed on them, and said unto them, Receive ye the Holy Ghost.

(The name Holy Ghost and Holy Spirit, are one in the same). John 20:22 is probably one of the most misunderstood scriptures there is. It says when Jesus breathed on His disciples and said receive the Holy Spirit, that was when they accepted Him, not when they actually received the baptism of the Holy Spirit.

Acts 1:4-5 And, being assembled together with them, commanded them that they should not depart from Jerusalem, but wait for the promise of the Father, which, saith he, ye have heard of me. For John truly baptized with water; but ye shall be baptized with the Holy Ghost not many days hence.

Acts 1:8 But ye shall receive power, after that the Holy Ghost is come upon you: and ye shall be witnesses unto me both in Jerusalem, and in all Judae'a, and in Samaria, and unto the uttermost part of the earth.

Acts 8:14-16 Now when the apostles which were at Jerusalem heard that Samaria had received the word of God, they sent unto them Peter and John: Who, when they were come down, prayed for them, that they might receive the Holy Ghost: (For as yet he was fallen upon none of them: only they were baptized in the name of the Lord Jesus.)

Acts 19:2-6 He said unto them, Have ye received the Holy Ghost since ye believed? And they said unto him, We have not so much as heard whether there be any Holy Ghost. And he said unto them, Unto what then were ye baptized? And they said, Unto John's baptism. Then said Paul, John verily baptized with the baptism of repentance, saying unto the people, that they should believe on him which should come after him, that is, on Christ Jesus. When they heard this, they were baptized in the name of the Lord Jesus. And when Paul had laid his hands upon them, the Holy Ghost came on them; and they spake with tongues, and prophesied.

Matthew 3:13 Then cometh Jesus from Galilee to Jordan unto John, to be baptized of him.

Matthew 3:16 And Jesus, when he was baptized, went up straightway out of the water: and, lo, the heavens were opened unto him, and he saw the Spirit of God descending like a dove, and lighting upon him.

If Jesus needed the baptism of the Holy Spirit, then we certainly do too. The only requirement is that you must first receive Jesus as Lord and believe in your heart that God our Father is faithful to give us what He has promised. God wants us to be baptized with His Holy Spirit; this is just one of the reasons that He sent us His only begotten Son.

RECEIVE THE BAPTISM OF THE HOLY SPIRIT

PRAY OUT LOUD

Father I realize that I need your power in my life. Please baptize me with your Holy Spirit. I believe that I receive Him right now! Holy Spirit you are welcome in my life. Thank you Father in Jesus name.

If you felt something happen or not, it doesn't really matter; the Holy Spirit now lives in your born again Spirit. Your spirit is the true you! This is the part of you that is saved, and will live forever. You are now one with Jesus and the Holy Spirit.

Ephesians 4:5-6 One Lord, one faith, one baptism, One God and Father of all, who is above all, and through all, and in you all.

One of the gifts you receive when baptized with the Holy Spirit is the ability to speak in tongues. This gift is a supernatural language from God that comes with the baptism of the Holy Spirit! Please don't be afraid of this because many churches have been deceived into thinking that this gift is not from God. However, there are some scriptures that disprove that lie. The Apostle Paul gives this command to the church:

1 Corinthians 14:39 Wherefore, brethren, covet to prophesy, and forbid not to speak in tongues.

1 Corinthians 14:18-19 I thank my God, I speak with tongues more than ye all: Yet in the church I had rather speak five words with my understanding, that by my voice I might teach others also, than ten thousand words in an unknown tongue.

What Paul is saying here is that the gift of speaking in tongues is mainly used to encourage ourselves by stirring us up in the Holy Spirit. Paul is also pointing out that if we are praying in tongues in a place where people are gathered together, they are not going to be able to understand what you are saying, and that it would be better for them if you were to have prophesied to them.

Praying or speaking in tongues also releases our faith because it is the Holy Spirit in us that's praying. We may not always know what, or even how to pray correctly, but the Holy Spirit knows exactly what to pray, He prays a perfect prayer every time. If you have just received the baptism of the Holy Spirit, then you have this gift in you.

The Holy Spirit isn't going to take control over you and start speaking against your will. He will only speak if you want Him to and only when you start speaking. You just have to decide OK let's do this, start praying or talking to God and at first you may only get one word or maybe just one syllable. This will be a language you probably won't recognize, it's coming from your spirit. Don't stop; keep repeating whatever you have said, even if it's only one word or syllable. As you keep doing this your language will increase. When you start speaking in your heavenly language you are releasing Gods presence from within your Spirit. This is extremely powerful. The devil will try to stop you by putting thoughts in your head like this is silly you are not making any sense. The reason behind him wanting to stop you is because you are releasing the power of the Holy Spirit, and that is a real threat to him. Another reason the devil doesn't like us speaking in tongues is because he can't understand anything were saying! This is a heavenly language that God has hidden from the enemy so that God can reveal His plans to you without any interference.

If for some reason you are having a hard time getting your language to come forth don't get upset, and don't give up, it doesn't mean that you didn't receive the baptism of the Holy Spirit, keep trying, it's well worth it!

If you continue to have difficulties then ask someone who does speak in tongues to help you. We operate in the gifts by faith and how faith works is by believing that you've already got it!

Jude 20 But ye, beloved, building up yourselves on your most holy faith, praying in the Holy Ghost.

Matthew 10:20 For it is not ye that speak, but the Spirit of your Father which speaketh in you.

Romans 8:26 Likewise the Spirit also helpeth our infirmities: for we know not what we should pray for as we ought: but the Spirit itself maketh intercession for us with groanings which cannot be uttered.

We must focus our attention on Christ in us, because we can do nothing on our own. But we are never alone! His miracle working power is released by faith and acknowledging that we have Christ in us and that He dwells in our born again spirit. Faith is the bridge that brings this power across from the spirit realm into the natural realm. It's Christ in us that does the greater works.

Philemon 1:6 That the communication of thy faith may become effectual by the acknowledging of every good thing which is in you in Christ Jesus.

1 John 5:4 For whatsoever is born of God overcometh the world: and this is the victory that overcometh the world, even our faith.

Hebrews 11:6 But without faith it is impossible to please him: for he that cometh to God must believe that he is, and that he is a rewarder of them that diligently seek him.

So how do we build up our faith, and release it? The first thing we need to know is that we are using the faith of Christ that is in our born again spirit, not our natural faith. Our natural faith on its own will not produce a supernatural effect, it only enables us to operate in our natural talents. It tells us things like I know that I can sit in a chair because my faith tells me that it's strong enough to support me.

Our natural faith can sometimes be enhanced by the supernatural faith of Christ in us. An example of this would be seen in something like artwork, creative writing or designing things. Supernatural faith is one of the fruits of the Spirit, listed in Galatians 5:22. We also see faith as one of the gifts of the Holy Spirit in 1 Corinthians 12:9.

In order for us to activate our supernatural faith, we must first stir up the Holy Spirit in us. There are different ways in which we can do this. The best way to start is by thanking Him, praising Him and acknowledging every good thing that we already have in us because He is capable of doing all things. All we really need to do is to agree to let Him work through us.

CHAPTER 2

Who Do You Say That I Am?

⚜

Genesis 1:26-28 And God said, Let us make man in our image, after our likeness: and let them have dominion over the fish of the sea, and over the fowl of the air, and over the cattle, and over all the earth, and over every creeping thing that creepeth upon the earth. So God created man in his own image, in the image of God created he him; male and female created he them. And God blessed them, and God said unto them, Be fruitful, and multiply, and replenish the earth, and subdue it: and have dominion over the fish of the sea, and over the fowl of the air, and over every living thing that moveth upon the earth.

WHEN GOD SAID, LET US make man in our image, after our likeness, He was talking to Jesus His Son and the Holy Spirit: God is a Spirit, a three part being, consisting of Father, Son, and Holy Spirit. So God created man, (male and female) in His own image: He created us also as a three part being, spirit, soul, and body.

Genesis 2:7 And the LORD God formed man of the dust of the ground, and breathed into his nostrils the breath of life; and man became a living Soul.

James 2:26 For as the body without the spirit is dead…

We know now that God is a three part being, and that we were created in His image! We were spoken into existence. James 2:26 shows us that our physical body is not able to live without the spirit. The Spirit is the breath of life.

1 Thessalonians 5:23 And the very God of peace sanctify you wholly; and I pray God your whole spirit and soul and body be preserved blameless unto the coming of our Lord Jesus Christ.

Hebrews 12:23 To the general assembly and church of the firstborn, which are written in heaven, and to God the Judge of all, and to the spirits of just men made perfect.

John 3:5 Jesus answered, Verily, verily, I say unto thee, Except a man be born of water and of the Spirit, he cannot enter into the kingdom of God.

When we received Jesus our spirit was completely changed.

2 Corinthians 5:17 Therefore if any man be in Christ, he is a new creature: old things are passed away; behold, all things are become new.

John 3:6 That which is born of the flesh is flesh; and that which is born of the Spirit is spirit.

We have already received everything that we will ever need. We now have all fullness of Him in our Spirit!

1 Corinthians 3:16 Know ye not that ye are the temple of God, and that the Spirit of God dwelleth in you?

John 1:16 And of his fullness have all we received, and grace for grace.

Colossians 1:27 To whom God would make known what is the riches of the glory of this mystery among the Gentiles; which is Christ in you, the hope of glory.

Colossians 2:9-10 For in him dwelleth all the fullness of the Godhead bodily. And ye are complete in him, which is the head of all principality and power.

Your born again Spirit is the same right now as it will be through all eternity! And if you have received the baptism of the Holy Spirit, then you have been given power from on high. You have the fullness of God in you! You have also received the spiritual Gifts of the Spirit: that are listed in 1 Corinthians chapter 12.

You also have a new nature, your character or personality of who you are now in your spirit is the same as Gods nature, He refers to them as the fruit of the Spirit.

Galatians 5:22-23 But the fruit of the Spirit is love, joy, peace, longsuffering, gentleness, goodness, faith, Meekness, temperance: against such there is no law.

Everything we could ever need has already been provided for us through the finished works of the cross. This is where most of the modern day church is missing it. Instead they are asking

God for more of Himself, or to pour out His Spirit on us, or reach down and touch us, or "Oh God we need you to show up here and do something, send revival." This attitude of begging and pleading with God, trying to get Him to do something that He has already done, profits you nothing! God wants us to talk to Him, like He's your friend and Father. As your friend you should treat Him with more respect than someone that you are just trying to get something from. I feel it's important to say that not only should He be your very best friend, but much more than that; we need to see our relationship with Him as more important than anything else, or anyone else, including ourselves.

> *Galatians 2:20 I am crucified with Christ: nevertheless I live; yet not I, but Christ liveth in me: and the life which I now live in the flesh I live by the faith of the Son of God, who loved me, and gave himself for me.*

> *Matthew 16:24-25 Then said Jesus unto his disciples, If any man will come after me, let him deny himself, and take up his cross, and follow me. For whosoever will save his life shall lose it: and whosoever will lose his life for my sake shall find it.*

What does it mean that a man should take up his cross? A cross is something you die to; when you make Jesus the Lord of your life, you need to mean it! You need to submit to Him, let Him lead, rule and reign in your life. Trust in the Lord to teach you and guide you in everything! Not just some things, once in awhile, part of the time, but rather in everything, all of the time.

The most important thing we can ever do is to get to know Him and to start to develop a deep relationship with Him.

Perhaps you may ask yourself how can I possibly be able to get to know God as my best friend? Easy, through our Lord Jesus. It might surprise you to know that this is what God wants. In fact He wants this even more than you do! That's what He created you for. He has a plan for your life that's way bigger than you could ever imagine.

> *John 14:6 Jesus saith unto him, I am the way, the truth, and the life: no man cometh unto the Father, but by me.*

> *Revelation 3:20-21 Behold, I stand at the door, and knock: If any man hear my voice, and open the door, I will come in to him, and will sup with him, and he with me. To him that overcometh will I grant to sit with me in my throne, even as I also overcame, and am set down with my Father in his throne.*

> *Matthew 6:33 But seek ye first the kingdom of God, and his righteousness; and all these things shall be added unto you.*

One of the biggest mistakes we make is to first try to get things from God before we ever begin to know Him. Stop and just think about this for a while, because it's way more important than just getting your needs met.

If you feel like you need to repent of something regarding your relationship with the Lord, then I encourage you to do so. Repenting really means to make a commitment of turning away from whatever it is that you don't want in your life that could hinder or hold you back from developing a deeper relationship with God.

Ask the Holy Spirit to help you with this, the Holy Spirit wants more than anything for you to ask Him to help you to grow in this journey of developing a closer relationship with God. If for some reason you ever feel like you messed up and have gotten off track, then stop and say, "Father I am sorry, I got off track somehow. Holy Spirit would you please help me to focus on Jesus, and to get back on track!" Remember that God has already forgiven you of all your sins, past, present and future. He has placed all of His wrath upon Jesus!

Many people are teaching these days that if you sin you could lose your salvation, and others are teaching that God won't bless you, or use you, until you confess your sin, and get it covered under the blood of Jesus. Neither one of those statements are true! They do not line up with scripture, and certainly do not recognize the one time sacrifice that Jesus made for us on the cross.

Hebrews 7:27 Who needed not daily, as those high priest, to offer up sacrifice, first for his own sin, and then for the people's: for this he did once, when he offered up himself.

Hebrews 10:10-12 By the which will we are sanctified through the offering of the body of Jesus Christ once for all. And every priest standeth daily ministering and offering oftentimes the same sacrifices, which can never take away sins: But this man, after he had offered one sacrifice for sins for ever, sat down on the right hand of God.

I am not saying that it's okay for us to sin now because Jesus has paid for our sins, past, present and future. NO certainly not! Sin will open up a door to the enemy, and he will take advantage of that any way he can. If you do sin, stop it now and repent of it!

Simply say, "I'm sorry Lord, I know that you have already forgiven me and that you have forgotten about all of my mistakes, and that you want me to forget about this and don't think about it anymore." Now take your authority over this unwanted thought, and cast it out, and replace it with good, pure, kingdom of God thoughts. Try to focus on these scriptures:

1 John 4:4 Ye are of God, little children, and have overcome them: because greater is he that is in you, than he that is in the world.

Romans 6:14-15 For sin shall not have dominion over you: for ye are not under the law, but under grace. What then? shall we sin, because we are not under the law, but under grace? God forbid.

Another way that I've learned to clear my head of any unwanted thoughts is to think of a song. If for some reason that doesn't work I put on a cd and just listen to music or a teaching I like. It really is up to us to decide if we want to continue allowing a thought to remain in our head, or not. We have authority over our thoughts and we can take them under control.

2 Corinthians 10:4-5 (For the weapons of our warfare are not carnal, but mighty through God to the pulling down of strongholds;) Casting down imaginations, and every high thing that exalteth itself against the knowledge of God, and bringing into captivity every thought to the obedience of Christ.

I picture a thought as words that are written down on a note pad, I can then take my hand and grab that page, where that thought is written and rip that page out, wad it up in my fist and cast it down. If it comes back, I say no you don't, and I pull that page off too. This way of seeing how to take thoughts captive is something that I can imagine myself doing. If this works for you then use it, or ask the Lord to show you a way that works better for you!

It's always best to get your own revelation from the Lord rather than having to depend upon someone else's insight on how we should receive what the Lord has for us. Although some of the things we learn from others can really help us.

However there are some teachings that will steer you in the wrong direction! I've heard people say that there's always going to be some meat (good stuff) and some bones (bad stuff) in whatever type of message is being presented to us, whether it is something we either hear, or read. They say to just eat the meat, and spit out the bones! Although there may be some truth to that, it is never a good idea to have a diet that has a bunch of bones in it! You may say to yourself, well I know what the truth is I can spit out the boney part and it won't have any effect on me! Not so! Everything we hear, read, or watch has somewhat of an impact on us. If you were listening to something you did not agree with, you would have to continually be saying to yourself, "I reject that in Jesus name" in order to keep that seed from growing.

There are plenty of things in the world that we are exposed to in everyday life that we really should be rejecting because they are painting a picture in your mind. Watching TV may seem harmless but it can be one of the most damaging things you could ever do, because it impresses an image in your brain, and if you don't reject this it will begin to start planting a seed. Words form pictures in your mind. If you were to think of a car you would see a picture of a car in your mind, not the word CAR. Suppose someone were to say to you think of a pie, you might see in your mind a apple pie, or a berry pie you don't see the word

PIE. Our imagination is something we all use every day. It even works when we are sleeping.

God gave us imagination so we could get through everyday life. We need this gift if we want to build something. It would be impossible to build a house without first looking at the plans. In order for someone to be able to draw a blueprint of that plan, you must first imagine what you want your house to look like; you then present your plan to an architect who also uses his imagination to help you design your home. It's kind of like faith, we can come in to agreement with someone and mix our faith, or in this case imaginations together to accomplish something. Imagination can be used in both a positive or negative way.

Could it be that if imagination were to be used by the people of the world, who are not born again believers, the result could lead to a corrupt and unjust society? Is the advertising industry using this to entice people into spending money? Has TV, movies, internet, magazines and even music, given people a sense of false identity, by putting thoughts in their heads, that maybe they could be like someone else, perhaps someone famous, rich, good looking or rebellious. Everybody is searching for something, a way that will make them look good and be noticed.

Romans 1:21 Because that, when they knew God, they glorified him not as God, neither were thankful; but became vain in their imaginations, and their foolish heart was darkened.

We only see the word imagination used three times in the New Testament. *(Luke 1:51, Romans 1:21, 2Corinthians 10:5).* All of these scriptures are warning us not to use imagination in an ungodly way.

Every day for about a week while I was eating my lunch, I listened to a teaching on imagination. One day after lunch I had some spare time so I asked the Holy Spirit to open the eyes of my understanding, and to help me focus on using my imagination. I prayed in tongues for a little while then I said to Him, "I am just going to lay still and listen to you." I had my eyes closed and I saw a small airplane, it was moving very fast in a straight line then it turned to the left. I could see this plane so clearly that I could even see the running lights. I knew that I was not asleep and dreaming, and that this was a vision, I asked the Lord why did you show me this airplane? I wasn't even thinking about a plane. After about five minutes, while I was waiting for an answer, I heard a loud sound of a engine. I sat up and looked out the window, I then saw this same plane fly past my house, real fast and turn to the left, the only difference was that it was day light, and I did not see any running lights. He showed me that if you can first see or know something in the spirit then you will see it in the natural realm.

We see in 2 Corinthians 10:4-5 that our imagination is a place where strongholds are formed, and we also know that it's in our minds where we do warfare. The only way that we can ever be attacked spiritually, is through our thoughts. We can't keep unwanted thoughts from coming at us, but we certainly can reject them in Jesus name! It's only when we allow these thoughts to become part of our imagination that they develop into strongholds. Thank God that Jesus has stripped all power and authority from the entire demonic realm, and has chosen to share this authority with us.

Colossians 2:15 And having spoiled principalities and powers, he made a shew of them openly, triumphing over them in it.

Matthew 28:18 And Jesus came and spake unto them, saying, All power is given unto me in heaven and in earth.

The authority we have been given is only to be used on this earth! We do not have authority over heavenly realms. Many people have over stepped their authority in this area and have opened up a door that should have never been opened. The battlefield is in your mind, through your thoughts. You do not have to fly somewhere in the spirit to do spiritual warfare, this goes way past the point of being stupid! Its dangerous don't do it. The enemy will be more than happy to take you some place in the spirit. But you said that the devil and all his hosts have been stripped of all power, and authority? Yes I did, and yes he has. However, if you come in to agreement with him, then you have just given the devil and all of his demons a right to mess with you.

The Lord showed me in a dream, that we should never let anyone take us to Heaven. He said that we should only allow Him, Jesus or Holy Spirit to take us to Heaven! Even if someone is a well know Christian, they can still be deceived. One day I was by myself eating lunch and I asked the Lord, "So if satan can give us a bad dream, then can he give us a vision?" The Lord said, "He took me to the pinnacle of the temple." *(Luke 4:9-Mathew 4:5).*

When we can first see or know something in the Spirit realm, that produces hope. When we mix that hope with faith then it will come to pass and we will see it in the natural realm. What if you needed healing in your body; if you can first imagine or see yourself healed, then all you have to do is just stand firm on that, believing it's something you already have in your spirit.

To stand believing is faith! Faith is engaged by speaking! This is what brings things from your spirit out into your physical body. Imagine your spirit, your innermost man as being full of Gods power; now imagine that power is in the form of living water inside you. Think of your mind as being a pump, and when you stand believing in faith, and speak forth the truth that God has revealed to you, this is what turns on the pump. It will flood your entire body with this living water; it's the power of God. If you were to leave the pump on for a while it would fill you to the point of overflow, and it will never run dry, it is an endless supply, a continuous flow from the river of life. Once you are filled with the Holy Spirit of God you will never need to be filled again.

We really need to stop messing around with all this unbelief about having to get another baptism of the Holy Spirit, or be refilled over and over again, or even worse we need Him to show up here because He never gave us enough in the first place. This way of thinking profits you nothing, this is what will either turn the pump completely off, or severely restrict the flow. This is exactly why America needs a wake-up call!

If for some reason you think that God did not give you enough of Himself or His power, then you are seeing yourself from a place of lack! And that will limit the flow of God's power through you. If we only knew how much power God has already placed in our born again spirit, we could change the world. If someone else is around you it will get on them too. The same way that you can see yourself healed is the same way you can see yourself prosperous, or delivered from anything that's oppressing you.

We need to know who we are in Christ before we can expect to ever flow in the power and authority He has given us.

We are over comers! We come from victory! We are sons and daughters of Almighty God! We have a loving Father that has given us everything we will ever need through His Son Jesus. It's simply believing and putting your trust in Him.

CHAPTER 3

Rock Solid Foundation

❖

Matthew 16:18 And I say also unto thee, That thou art Peter, and upon this rock I will build my church; and the gates of hell shall not prevail against it.

JESUS ASKED HIS DISCIPLES, "WHO do you say that I am," and Peter answered and said, "You are the Christ, the Son of the living God."

Matthew 16:17 And Jesus answered and said unto him, Blessed art thou, Simon Barjo'na: for flesh and blood hath not revealed it unto thee, but my Father which is in heaven.

When Jesus said to Peter, "and upon this rock I will build my church", Jesus is talking about the relationship that will be re-established between us and God our Father. Once Jesus went to the cross, the relationship Adam and Eve had has now been and is forever re-established through Jesus, and that through Him everyone will be able to hear from God.

John 14:6 Jesus saith unto him, I am the way, the truth, and the life: no man cometh unto the Father, but by me.

Most people don't seem to realize that there is a huge difference between being under the old covenant, which is referred to as being under the Law, and the new covenant, or New Testament, which is a covenant of grace. The new covenant could also be described as the finished works of the cross. Through the shed blood of Jesus we can now enter into a rest because Jesus has fulfilled all of the requirements of the Old Testament law. Rest simply means that we no longer have to go through performance based works before God will grant us a blessing.

> *Hebrews 4:9-11 There remaineth therefore a rest to the people of God. For he that is entered into his rest, he also hath ceased from his own works, as God did from his. Let us labour therefore to enter into that rest, lest any man fall after the same example of unbelief.*

All of this stuff about you have to first be holy and do everything just right or God won't bless you is all an old covenant way of doing things. It's nothing more than a bunch of religious works. Trying to live according to the old covenant law will only make you frustrated and leave you feeling stuck and unsatisfied. We need to know that we are no longer bound by the law we are now under grace.

We see in Genesis that God ceased from all His work that He had created in six days and on the seventh day He rested. Even in the Old Testament God commanded that the seventh day was to be a Holy day of rest. Now that we are under the new covenant of grace we can see that God is telling us that we are to enter into a rest from our works of trying to earn God's favor. Jesus has already done all the work and it is finished.

Hebrews 4:5-6 And in this place again, If they shall enter into my rest. Seeing therefore it remaineth that some must enter therein, and they to whom it was first preached entered not in because of unbelief.

God wants us to know that if we are to labor for anything it is to learn more about who Jesus is and how much He has done for us. Jesus is our rock, He is our solid foundation. He is the way, the truth and the life.

Once you come to a place of knowing who you are in Christ then you can enter into a seven day a week rest! This rest is a gift and the only way you can get it is to learn how to grow in the knowledge of Him through a relationship with Him. When you have gotten to this point of knowing your identity in Christ, then you can have what you ask for. God does not want us to be like the Israelites who could not enter into His rest because of their unbelief. God has given us His word so that we can live a life of victory and Jesus is our perfect example of how we should live our lives.

Jesus has completely stripped the enemy of all their power and authority! Don't pray and ask Jesus to come down here and rebuke the devil for you, He's already won that fight. Jesus is in you and has given you His authority. He expects you to partner with Him and use the authority that He has given you. Remember that deliverance has already been provided for us as one of the finished works of the cross. As New Testament believers we have already been given all the power and authority that we are ever going to get.

Once you are born again and baptized in the Holy Spirit you never have to worry about your prayers being blocked from getting up into heaven. We now have Jesus and the Holy Spirit living inside of us, He always hears us. The only way that we can now be hindered from receiving whatever we need is through our thought process. Our thoughts must be on things that are true, such as the word of God. The power that is in our spirit is the Holy Spirit in us, it's Christ in us.

The only way that we can release that power is through our mind or soul realm. Our thoughts need to bear witness with the Holy Spirit who lives in us. Once we know the truth of what God's word says and by faith start speaking forth that truth, then that is when the power of the Holy Spirit can be released from within us out into our mind and then into our body.

This is why satan puts thoughts of doubt and unbelief in your head to try and hinder you from receiving the things that God has for you. This is also why we need to renew our mind to line up with the word of God.

The only way that the enemy can afflict us with anything is by tricking us into thinking that there is something wrong with us, and then if we start believing that lie and speaking it forth, we will have what we say.

An example of this would be if you were starting to feel depressed, unworthy, or condemned about mistakes you have made in the past. This kind of thing is not from God. It can seem very real and it can become real if you don't start taking authority over it and speaking to it out loud, and commanding it to leave in Jesus name! If it tries to come back don't listen to it, instead start thanking and praising the Lord. If you don't pay any attention to those lying spirits, then they will give up and leave.

James 4:7 Submit yourselves therefore to God. Resist the devil, and he will flee from you.

Another way that the enemy gains access to us is through sin. When we sin we are coming into agreement with the enemy. It's an open door for him to step through. Repent from that sin, and use your authority against whatever it is that's attacking you. Most all types of sickness and disease are demonic. Use your authority that Jesus has given you and speak right to this afflicting spirit just like you were talking to another person! Do not carry on a conversation with a demonic spirit and don't ask them what their name is. Only give commands that are short and to the point. Never command a demon to leave someone more than once. If you were to repeatedly say to a demon I cast you out, that demon is going to know that if you said this a second time that you are operating in unbelief because you did not believe it yourself the first time you spoke. Command the attack to stop now, take authority over the spirit that is causing this affliction and command it to leave now in Jesus name. You can also say, "I cancel the assignment of any demon that is hindering me in Jesus name!" These are just a few examples of what to do.

You really need to follow the leading of the Holy Spirit on this. If you are ministering to another person then never cast a demon out of a person that is not born again, they do not have the authority to keep themselves free from these demonic spirits. If these spirits were to come back and they certainly can, then that person who was set free could wind up in an even worse condition. Always minister to someone first and tell them about Jesus and what He has done for us and the authority He has given us as believers to use His name so that we can be set free. Try to point out to that person just how important it is to be born again and let them make their own choice. It is also important for you to know that someone has to first want to be set free from some demonic influence in order for it to work. This has to do with the free will which we all have been given. This free will is a powerful force which we should not override without their permission.

Luke 11:24-26 When the unclean spirit is gone out of a man, he walketh through dry places, seeking rest; and finding none, he saith, I will return unto my house whence I came out. And when he cometh, he findeth it swept and garnished. Then goeth he, and taketh to him seven other spirits more wicked than himself; and they enter in, and dwell there: and the last state of that man is worse than the first.

The scripture listed above is talking about a person who is not born again. A person who has become demon possessed is someone who has a demon in their spirit that's controlling them. As we discussed earlier when you are born again your spirit is changed and is now cleansed made righteous, pure and holy. Your spirit was also sealed so that no demon can penetrate that seal. Your spirit is the part of you that was saved, or born again, not your body. Your body is separate from your spirit it is the housing or outer shell. Just because the spirit lives inside your body that does not mean that your body is holy and sanctified. Even a born again Christian can have demonic spirits in their body. That is why we see born again Christians who are sick and afflicted with disease. This is why Jesus has given us authority to come against these unclean spirits and cast them out.

Luke 10:19-20 Behold, I give unto you power to tread on serpents and scorpions, and over all the power of the enemy: and nothing shall by any means hurt you. Notwithstanding in this rejoice not, that the spirits are subject unto you; but rather rejoice, because your names are written in heaven.

In Luke 10:20 Jesus gives us a good word of advice by saying rejoice not that the spirits are subject to you. What Jesus is telling us is that we should not spend most of our time focusing on taking authority over these evil spirits. We do not have to spend a lot of time coming against the things that the devil is trying to send toward us. Only use the authority that you have been given when it's necessary not just because you can.

If you were to spend the majority of your time doing spiritual warfare, fighting and rebuking the devil, then you are not spending your time focusing on God and His kingdom. When we spend time focusing on God, Jesus and the Holy Spirit then we are empowering the kingdom of God in our lives. If we find ourselves spending most of our time thinking about satan and his kingdom then we are empowering the enemy because we are not giving our attention to Jesus. Jesus is the one who has empowered us to be able to operate within the kingdom of God.

Ephesians 4:8 Wherefore he saith, When he ascended up on high, he led captivity captive, and gave gifts unto men.

Matthew 12:29 Or else how can one enter into a strong man's house, and spoil his goods, except he first bind the strong man? and then he will spoil his house.

Acts 19:13-16 Then certain of the vagabond Jews, exorcists, took upon them to call over them which had evil spirits the name of the Lord Jesus, saying, We adjure you by Jesus whom Paul preacheth. And there were seven sons of one Sceva, a Jew, and chief of the priests, which did so. And the evil spirit answered and said, Jesus I know, and Paul I know; but who are ye? And the man in whom the evil spirit was leaped on them, and overcame them, and prevailed against them, so that they fled out of that house naked and wounded.

I have had people question me because I said that you should never cast demons out of people who are not saved. They bring up a good point. They say Jesus cast demons out of people before they were born again and this is true. Jesus not only cast these demons out but He gave His disciples authority to cast out demons. Jesus was able to operate in all the gifts of the Holy Spirit without having anything that could hinder Him in any way. He was a man without sin He had no doubt or unbelief. Jesus said He only did what He saw His Father do so we know that Jesus was so well tuned into hearing and seeing what God His Father wanted to say or do that He was able to perfectly minister to that person.

I believe that Jesus instantly knew what was on His Fathers heart. We never see where Jesus told people to come back later because He needed to go and pray before He could help them. I also believe that Jesus was able to impart this knowing ability to hear from God to His disciples so that they were able to minister to people in a way that would be most beneficial to them. Because Jesus was among His disciples here on earth they were able to operate under His authority. When Jesus reappeared to His disciples for the last time, He told them He was going to His father and that He would send the Comforter. He told them to go to Jerusalem and wait there until they receive power from on high when the Holy Spirit is sent to abide with them.

Upon this Rock I will build my church, and the gates of hell shall not prevail against it. Jesus is our rock. He is our solid foundation. He's done it all for us when He went to the cross for us and said it is finished! What we need is to grow in the knowledge of Him who has reconciled us back to a place of right standing relationship. The best way to gain knowledge is to read His word and to spend time with Him, talk to Him and then listen. I find its better to spend more time listening than talking. You are not going to hear from God when you are the one doing all the talking. It's should be a two way conversation, so shut up and listen to what the Spirit of the Lord has to say!

Psalms 46:10 Be still, and know that I am God: I will be exalted among the heathen, I will be exalted in the earth.

This is what it's all about. We must be able to hear from God, He is always willing to talk to us and tell us what's on His heart. When we don't hear from God it's not because He doesn't feel like talking, it's because where not tuned in to hearing Him. We need to get rid of all distractions; we need to unplug and turn everything off so we can pay attention. Background noise such as TV or a radio can make it real hard to focus. Spending a lot of time watching TV or on the computer playing games or looking at things that are not of God will dull your senses. The amount of time that you spend with the Lord has a lot to do with how much you are going to get out of this relationship. We can't just spend a few minutes a day praying in the morning and at night and then not even think about God the rest of the day. Neither should we expect to get what we need from just going to church on Sunday and spending the rest of the week occupied with doing our own thing and disregarding the things of God. That won't even come close to knowing what God's will is for your life. It's all about the relationship!

God speaks to us in many different ways. God can speak to us in an audible voice. I've had this happen to me four times. It's just like if you were talking to someone face to face, you can hear His voice out loud. He also reveals things to us through dreams and visions. Most of the time He just puts a thought in my head, it's like all of a sudden I just know something. This is probably the same way that Peter received a word of knowledge from God in knowing that Jesus was the Son of God.

I was involved in ministry with two healing rooms and I was attending a church, and I also was involved in a supernatural ministry school as an alumni. The Lord told me (this time it was a still small voice) to lay everything down, both healing rooms the church and the school. He wanted me to spend time with Him so I could grow in my relationship with Him. This really was an answer to my request in wanting to operate more in the spirit. I spent a lot of time just being still and listening. Other times I would pray, mostly in tongues. I also spent time soaking to some music that had no words, and a lot of time just reading the Bible and no other books. After about three months I just started to know things; it was like getting downloads of understanding scripture in more depth and detail.

I like to watch Andrew Wommack's TV show the Gospel Truth. I started getting confirmation through Andrew's show on all these thoughts and downloads that I had previously received from God. This went on for about another three months. It was a blessing to get confirmation on all this. However, the Lord asked me if I really needed to hear all of this again from Andrew. I learned that there is a greater blessing on those who only believe without having to get confirmation on everything, and will simply believe in faith.

We must know the word of God. We need to read His word in order to get to know Him. We can't just expect God to start speaking to us and downloading information to us without first seeking to know Him through reading His word. There are more benefits to knowing the word than we can possibly imagine. One of the ways that the enemy attacks us is through a lack of understanding of what the word of God says. Satan will question us regarding our knowledge of scripture. He tried this with Jesus in the wilderness, but that didn't work so well.

Matthew 4:3-4 And when the tempter came to him, he said, If thou be the Son of God, command that these stones be made bread. But he answered and said, It is written, Man shall not live by bread alone, but by every word that proceedeth out of the mouth of God.

Just because you hear a voice or have a thought that doesn't always mean that it came from God, this is why it is so important to know what the Bible says!

There are some ways by which we can tell if a voice or a thought came from God or not. Do you feel peace about this voice or thought? If not, then chances are it did not come from God. You may want to ask Him if it came from Him or not. Ask the Holy Spirit to help you operate in the gift of discerning of spirits about the thought or voice you heard. Try the spirit.

1 John 4:2-4 Hereby know ye the Spirit of God: Every spirit that confesseth that Jesus Christ is come in the flesh is of God: And every spirit that confesseth not that Jesus Christ is come in the flesh is not of God: and this is that spirit of antichrist, whereof ye have heard

that it should come; and even now already is it in the world. Ye are
of God, little children, and have overcome them: because greater is
he that is in you, than he that is in the world.

I know that trying the spirits works; I've done it many times. Just ask by saying, "The spirit that gave me this answer did Jesus come in the flesh?" You will either get a yes or no. You can also use this on words of prophesy that you get from other people as well.

Most of the people that I minister to could have probably been able to solve a lot of their own problems if they only knew who they were in Christ, that is to say, being strong in their identity. The other thing that they are missing is a clear understanding of how powerful they could be if they would only believe and trust in the authority Jesus has given them to use.

If we are going to make a difference in this world we need to have a deep understanding of who we have become in Jesus. Once we know that, there is no possible way that we could ever be moved from our position in Christ. We must not be double minded.

James 1:5-8 If any of you lack wisdom, let him ask of God, that
giveth to all men liberally, and upbraideth not; and it shall be given
him. But let him ask in faith, nothing wavering. For he that wa-
vereth is like a wave of the sea driven with the wind and tossed. For
let not that man think that he shall receive any thing of the Lord.
A double minded man is unstable in all his ways.

In your born again Spirit you have the mind of Christ that knows all things.

1 Corinthians 2:16 For who has known the mind of the Lord, that he may instruct him? But we have the mind of Christ.

1 John 2:20 But ye have an unction from the Holy one, and ye know all things.

We should never rely on what we see, hear or feel in the flesh because that is not a good source for knowing the truth. We should always be aware that this mind of Christ has been given to us because we have Christ in us and that we can have access to the truth and knowledge of Christ by simply asking. We have already been made so complete in our spirit that if we were ever able to get a good clear understanding of this then we would begin to understand that nothing is impossible.

Matthew 7:24-25 Therefore whosoever heareth these sayings of mine, and doeth them, I will liken him unto a wise man, which built his house upon a rock: And the rain descended, and the floods came, and the winds blew, and beat upon that house; and it fell not: for it was founded upon a rock.

CHAPTER 4

The Goodness of God

❖

WHEN WE COMPARE THE OLD Testament to the New Testament we
see what would appear to be a huge difference in how God relates
to people. Under the old covenant we see in certain places where
God is angry and pouring out His wrath upon His people. Then
under the new covenant of grace the Bible tells us that God is mer-
ciful, forgiving and kind.   He is a God of love and grace who is for
us and not against us.

In the Old Testament God commanded the people of Israel
to go into some of the neighboring villages within the Promised
Land where foreigners lived and to kill every one of them. In the
New Testament we see that Jesus not only heals a man, but Jesus
tells the man his sins have been forgiven.   So why do we see such
a difference? Did God change His mind about how He views us?
No, God didn't change. Instead He gave us a new covenant that
we now live under.

Malachi 3:6 For I am the LORD, I change not…

After Adam and Eve had eaten of the tree of knowledge of
good and evil, God could no longer allow them to stay in the
Garden of Eden because the tree of life was also there in the

garden and if they were to eat of the tree of life they would live forever in a fallen state of sin. What was even worse is that they would live forever in a state of being subjected to whatever kind of afflictions the devil had placed on them. Because God is good He did Adam and Eve a favor and kicked them out of the garden.

Genesis 3:23-24 Therefore the LORD God sent him forth from the garden of Eden, to till the ground from whence he was taken. So he drove out the man; and he placed at the east of the garden of Eden Cherubims, and a flaming sword which turned every way, to keep the way of the tree of life.

Since God is all powerful and is the creator of all things, why didn't He just fix this problem, after all He is the final authority and is sovereign above all things right? Yes, God is sovereign, He is the one in charge over all things, the absolute highest form of authority there is and ever will be. Yes, God could fix this problem but that would mean having to start over. If He were to start over then He would have had to completely dissolve everything that He had created, including Adam and Eve. When God spoke everything into existence, that spoken word became a substance that produced those things into the natural realm. God never goes back on His word. If for some reason God were to say, "I've changed my mind. I take back my word about all these things that I created, the heavens, the earth and all the host there of." If God were to do that then everything that we now see, and even the things that exist which we cannot see, would just dissolve. The only thing that would be left is God.

Genesis 1:1 In the beginning God created the heaven and the earth.

In the beginning there was only God. He had to first be there in order to create all these things. The Bible starts out by saying in the beginning, but it's referring to all things that pertain to us as we know them to be. Such as the heavens, the earth and all the host there of. Where the Bible says in the beginning it does not mean the beginning of God.

In the first chapter of Genesis we see that God gave dominion over the earth to Adam and Eve. Satan stole that dominion and the right to operate under that authority from Adam and Eve. There are always going to be consequences when we are disobedient to God's word. As we can plainly see by what happened to Adam and Eve, it's never a good idea to go against God's word. Although God gives us free will to make our own choices, it's up to us whether or not we take God's advice and follow His instructions. God will never force us to do anything that we don't want to do. God is more than willing to help us if we will turn to Him for guidance.

Because God has given us free will, He will never violate that right. God gave us free will hoping that we would recognize and receive the love that He has for us. Because God first loved us and commended His love toward us while we were yet sinners, He is hoping that we will choose to love Him in return. Before you ever turned your heart towards God, He loved you. However, you can never have a meaningful relationship with someone if you are trying to make that person love you, it just won't work. It's up to us to choose whether or not we want to have a relationship with God. If for some reason you think that you are not worthy of having a relationship with God, then I have good news for you! It doesn't matter what you may have done in the past or what you may even do in the future because Jesus paid for all your sins when He went to the cross! God is not judging you. He is not going to pour out His wrath on you. Neither is God judging this nation or any other nation because He poured out ALL of His wrath on Jesus.

Under the new covenant of grace if we were to sin it will not separate us from the love of God, neither will God judge you for it. Instead, what will happen is that you will subject yourself to the law of sowing and reaping.

> *Romans 8:35 Who shall separate us from the love of Christ? shall tribulation, or distress, or persecution, or famine, or nakedness, or peril, or sword?*

> *Romans 8:38-39 For I am persuaded, that neither death, nor life, nor angels, nor principalities, nor powers, nor things present, nor things to come, Nor height, nor depth, nor any other creature, shall be able to separate us from the love of God, which is in Christ Jesus our Lord.*

> *Galatians 6:7-8 Be not deceived; God is not mocked: for whatsoever a man soweth, that shall he also reap. For he that soweth to his flesh shall of the flesh reap corruption; but he that soweth to the Spirit shall of the Spirit reap life everlasting.*

Sin will open a door to the devil and you will reap corruption, it is a consequence of sowing bad seed. Many people have mistakenly taught that if you sin God is going to somehow punish you, or put some kind of sickness upon you. None of this is true. God is not the one who places sickness upon us; it's the devil that brings things like sickness and disease on us, not God. These teachings come from looking back at the Old Testament law. They see the affects of what sowing and reaping are now having on someone and they automatically think that it's Gods judgment being poured out on them, or they even go so far as to say that God is judging an entire nation. There will come a day when God will judge every nation, but that day has not come yet, we are still living under a covenant of grace.

Sinning is a stupid thing to do and it is not who you are now. It will cause you problems so don't do it. You are no longer a sinner, you are a new creation the old things have passed away all things have become new.

> *1 John 2:1 My little children, these things write I unto you, that ye sin not. And if any man sin, we have an advocate with the Father, Jesus Christ the righteous.*

> *2 Corinthians 5:17 Therefore if any man be in Christ, he is a new creature: old things are passed away; behold, all things are become new.*

Was God so mad at Adam and Eve for being disobedient that He separated Himself from them and no longer wanted anything to do with them? No certainly not. He still loved them and talked with them. However, the level in which they could now experience God's presence had been severely compromised. Where they once had a relationship of oneness with God without anything hindering them, they now had to deal with all these new negative thoughts of evil things that they never had before. But what was even worse was their supernatural gift of faith that they had of being connected as one and in right standing with God was now compromised and hindered by satan's lies and negative thoughts. They still were in relationship with God but it was just a long distance relationship. Sin became that separation. The Bible says that Adam and Eve walked with God in the garden, but the Bible never says that they could see God with their physical eyes. I think that's because they walked with God in the Spirit by faith. I also believe that the spiritual realm was just as real to them as the natural realm was, because they had a completely pure sense of faith. It wasn't God who withdrew Himself from them. It was Adam and Eve who became separated from God by allowing sin to enter into their lives.

Adam and Eve had two sons, Cain and Abel. Abel was a keeper of sheep, but Cain was a tiller of the ground. Both Cain and Abel brought offerings to give to the Lord. And the Lord had respect for Abel's offering, but not for Cain's offering.

> *Genesis 4:6-8 And the LORD said unto Cain, Why art thou wroth? and why is thy countenance fallen? If thou doest well, shalt thou not be accepted? and if thou doest not well, sin lieth at the door. And unto thee shall be his desire, and thou shalt rule over him. And Cain talked with Abel his brother: and it came to pass, when they were in the field, that Cain rose up against Abel his brother, and slew him.*

We can see that God was still talking with both Cain and Abel, and that God even tries to warn Cain that when he starts getting mad at his brother he is opening himself up to sin by being tempted of satan. Notice that God spoke to Cain and tried to get him to stop and think about what would happen when you let anger in. God never forced Cain, He allowed Cain to still make his own decision even though it caused him to commit a sin that cost his brother Abel his life.

Romans 5:12-14 Wherefore, as by one man sin entered into the world, and death by sin; and so death passed upon all men, for that all have sinned: (For until the law sin was in the world: but sin is not imputed when there is no law. Nevertheless death reigned from Adam to Moses, even over them that had not sinned after the similitude of Adam's transgression, who is the figure of him that was to come.

Of course we should all know by now that the figure of Him that was to come is Jesus. While death reigned because of sin, that sin was not imputed unto man. That simply means God was not keeping track of the sins people were committing. During this period of time God had not yet given them the covenant of law. They were living under God's mercy at this time and God was blessing them and trying to help them, but they just kept on sinning since they knew that they could get away with it, and were not being punished for it. The lifestyle of sin that mankind was living with was getting worse.

Genesis 6:1-6 And it came to pass, when men began to multiply on the face of the earth, and daughters were born unto them, That the sons of God saw the daughters of men that they were fair; and they took them wives of all which they chose. And the LORD said, My spirit shall not always strive with man, for that he also is flesh: yet his days shall be an hundred and twenty years. There were giants in the earth in those days; and also after that, when the sons of God came in unto the daughters of men, and they bare children to them, the same became mighty men which were of old, men of renown. And God saw that the wickedness of man was great in the earth, and that every imagination of the thoughts of his heart was only evil continually. And it repented the LORD that he had made man on the earth, and it grieved him at his heart.

As people begin to multiply on the earth we see how some people are following after God and others were not. Some of the daughters of ungodly men were being taken as wives by godly men. This was a cause of wide spread corruption throughout the earth because these daughters that were taken as wives had turned men's hearts away from God and brought in idol worshiping, sexual immorality, etc.

It is truly amazing to see that God was regretting that He had ever made mankind and was planning to flood the entire earth. This confirms the fact that God will bless those that will follow Him with a pure heart. God told Noah that He had enough of mans corruption and that the earth was filled with violence and that He was going to destroy all flesh.

Genesis 6:17-18 And, behold, I, even I, do bring a flood of waters upon the earth, to destroy all flesh, wherein is the breath of life, from under heaven; and every thing that is in the earth shall die. But with thee will I establish my covenant; and thou shalt come into the ark, thou, and thy sons, and thy wife, and thy sons' wives with thee.

Genesis 7:11-12 In the six hundredth year of Noah's life, in the second month, the seventeenth day of the month, the same day were all the fountains of the great deep broken up, and the windows of heaven were opened. And the rain was upon the earth forty days and forty nights.

If God so loved Adam and Eve that He spared their lives after they had sinned then why do we see Him now flooding the earth and killing everyone who lived on it except for Noah and his family? God spared Adam and Eve because He loved them. God did not want to kill all these people in a flood; it was something He had to do. If He had not done anything at all then how much longer would it have been before Noah and his family became corrupt, or if not Noah and his immediate family then what about his descendants? We need to remember that it was the devil that was turning everybody away from God by filling their minds with evil thoughts. In the Old Testament people did not have authority over the demonic realm like we do as born again believers. Once people became demon possessed back then they could not get set free on their own, they were stuck that way. The only way to avoid this was to live a righteous life of being devoted to God. It's hard to imagine that throughout all the entire earth there were only eight righteous people left in Noah's day.

2 Peter 2:5 And spared not the old world, but saved Noah the eighth person, a preacher of righteousness, bringing in the flood upon the world of the ungodly.

We also see another place in scripture were God destroyed the two cities, Sodom and Gomorrah. The people in both of these cities had become so corrupt and evil that there was only one righteous family left there, a man named Lot, his wife and two daughters. Lot, who was the nephew of Abraham, lived in this place and God told Abraham He would bring judgment upon Sodom and Gomorrah. Abraham became concerned because he knew that his nephew Lot lived there. Abraham drew near to God.

Genesis 18:23-24 And Abraham drew near, and said, Wilt thou also destroy the righteous with the wicked? Peradventure there be fifty righteous within the city: wilt thou also destroy and not spare the place for the fifty righteous that are therein?

Abraham first starts out by asking God if He will not destroy this place if there are fifty righteous people there. When God says I won't destroy it because of the fifty people, then Abraham says well what about forty five people and again God says I won't destroy it if there are forty five righteous people. Once Abraham saw that he is able to change Gods mind about this he then tries for thirty and twenty he even goes down as far as ten people and he stops at that point. Maybe Abraham was thinking I better not press my luck on this any further than I already have!

Genesis 19:15 And when the morning arose, then the angels hastened Lot, saying, Arise, take thy wife, and thy two daughters, which are here; lest thou be consumed in the iniquity of the city.

Genesis 19:24 Then the LORD rained upon Sodom and upon Gomorrah brimstone and fire from the LORD out of heaven.

As we read through the Old Testament scriptures it would seem as though satan was causing a tremendous amount of trouble in the world and that God had to destroy entire cities. We also see from reading about Noah, that God had to almost completely start over because of the infiltration of all this sin which had infected almost the entire human race. Wouldn't it have been easier for God to have just hit the delete button on satan?

None of us have all the answers and God may have reasons for doing things that we don't fully understand, however, the Bible does give us some clues about these things. All of the angels including satan are a spirit, and are not subject to having to live in a physical body like we do; therefore they cannot die a physical death like we do. Even though we experience a physical death, our spirit will continue to live. It is only by the goodness of God that we are given a choice as to where we want to spend eternity. Hell is a real place that has been reserved for satan and all of those fallen angels who chose to follow him. Even the people who simply refuse to follow Jesus will end up there, even though it was <u>never</u> Gods intention that any of us should perish.

2 Peter 2:4 For if God spared not the angels that sinned, but cast them down to hell, and delivered them into chains of darkness, to be reserved unto judgment.

2 Peter 3:9 The Lord is not slack concerning his promise, as some men count slackness; but is longsuffering to us-ward, not willing that any should perish, but that all should come to repentance.

During the time span from Adam to Moses the Old Testament gives us insight as to how people were living their lives when God was not imputing their sins against them. They were not breaking any of Gods laws because no law had yet been given. We can plainly see that mankind is not capable of living a righteous life of self control and discipline. God had to do something to get mankind back on course so God gave them the law through Moses. God knew that the people of Israel needed to have their sins revealed to them and that they needed to be made aware just how destructive those sins were.

So God gave them His ten commandments. (*Exodus 20*). God also gave them many other divine laws to follow. God knew that the people of Israel would never be able to live up to the standards that He set before them. Therefore, God said to Moses that He was to establish a priest's office using his brother Aaron as the head of the priesthood and that once a year

Aaron could make a sacrifice of atonement for the sins of the people of Israel.

The wages of sin is death and God only allowed the priests of Israel to make sacrifices of animals to atone for the peoples sins. This shedding of the blood of animals was just a shadow of the things to come. Jesus was the Lamb of God that offered Himself as the one time final sacrifice that took away all the sins of the world that had been separating us from God!

> *Hebrews 9:28 So Christ was once offered to bear the sins of many; and unto them that look for him shall he appear the second time without sin unto salvation.*

> *Hebrews 7:26-27 For such an high priest became us, who is holy, harmless, undefiled, separate from sinners, and made higher than the heavens; Who needeth not daily, as those high priests, to offer up sacrifice, first for his own sins, and then for the people's: for this he did once, when he offered up himself.*

> *Hebrews 9:24-25 For Christ is not entered into the holy places made with hands, which are the figures of the true; but into heaven itself, now to appear in the presence of God for us: Nor yet that he should offer himself often, as the high priest entereth into the holy place every year with blood of others.*

Throughout the Old Testament and even in the four gospels we see that there are many things that point to the finished works of the cross. Many of the things that the prophets in the Old Testament spoke of were only just a shadow of things to come, they all point to the finished works of Jesus, His redemptive power of the cross and the fulfilling of the Old Testament law.

We really have an awesome future and not only can we start living in it right now, but we need to be thinking about how great it's going to be when we go to be with the Lord. This is all because we have a really good God who only wants what's best for us. God is all for us He wants us to grow in the knowledge of what He has for us. God is no longer angry with us like we have seen in the Old Testament. When God looks at us now He sees Jesus in us. He sees us now as His sons and daughters.

1 John 4:15-17 Whosoever shall confess that Jesus is the Son of God, God dwelleth in him, and he in God. And we have known and believed the love that God hath to us. God is love; and he that dwelleth in love dwelleth in God, and God in him. Herein is our love made perfect, that we may have boldness in the day of judgment: because as he is, so are we in this world.

John 3:16 For God so loved the world, that he gave his only begotten Son, that whosoever believeth in him should not perish, but have everlasting life.

CHAPTER 5

Grace and Faith

⚜

Ephesians 1:4-5 According as he has chosen us in him before the foundation of the world, that we should be holy and without blame before him in love: Having predestinated us unto the adoption of children by Jesus Christ to himself, according to the good pleasure of his will.

EVEN BEFORE YOU EVER EXISTED God had a plan for your life. He has a purpose for you being here on earth, a calling; we could say that He has a job just for you. It's not that we knew God before the foundation of the world, but rather that He had a predestinated plan of what we were to do in this life. We are to seek and pursue a relationship with God through Jesus. He will then reveal to you what He has planned for you, and how to start moving towards that goal.

Ephesians 2:10 For we are his workmanship, created in Christ Jesus unto good works, which God hath before ordained that we should walk in them.

Ephesians 1:11-12 In whom also we have obtained an inheritance, being predestinated according to the purpose of him who worketh all things after the counsel of his own will: That we should be to the praise of his glory, who first trusted in Christ.

By grace God has already made everything available to us that we will ever need to carry out the unique destiny which He has planned for each and every one of us. The scriptures say that God has hidden things <u>for</u> us, not from us. He calls those hidden things mysteries.

Ephesians 1:9 Having made known unto us the mystery of his will, according to his good pleasure which he hath purposed in himself.

Proverbs 25:2 It is the glory of God to conceal a thing: but the honour of kings is to search out a matter.

God wants you to discover what your destiny is that He has designed for your life. There are many ways in which God reveals things to us. He could speak to you in an audible voice. He may have somebody give you a word of prophecy. He may reveal these things to you through scripture or He can give you dreams and visions. God may use every single one of these ways to get His message across to you.

When He shows us the same thing two or more times it is because it's something that He has for us or that He wants us to know. God may have a plan for you that may include operating in multiple things; for example healing, teaching and deliverance. Once God starts revealing pieces of His plan to you then that is when you need to start asking Him to help you and to give you instruction on where to begin. God is not going to reveal His plan to you all at once. He wants you to grow one step at a time until He knows that you are ready to take the next step. God does not want you to step out on your own into anything until you are ready. We need to wait for God to tell us when we are ready it's all on His timing, not ours.

You cannot make God do anything and you cannot persuade God by begging and pleading with Him to use you. He will show you what you need to learn then He will tell you when you are ready to be used. God has already anointed us and blessed us with all spiritual blessings. We just need to discover what that anointing is and learn how to grow in it.

Ephesians 1:3 Blessed be the God and Father of our Lord Jesus Christ, who hath blessed us with all spiritual blessings in heavenly places in Christ.

God poured out His Spirit on us after we were born again and received the baptism of the Holy Spirit. This is when you received all of the Spiritual blessings and all the anointing that you were ever going to need. Notice that this verse points out where all these blessings are; they are in Christ and He is in us!

All of the blessings, power and anointing that we will ever need have already been provided by grace! It is a free gift from God that was bought and paid for by Jesus. Most people have been taught that your faith is what moves God. That's not how it works. You cannot get God to move and do something. Don't expect that all of these Spiritual gifts and blessings are just going to fall out of heaven onto your lap like a bunch of ripe cherries. We need to learn how to access what we have in our spirit. The only way we can do that is through faith. Your faith will only move you into a place of receiving the things that God has already provided by grace. The word grace is describing the things God has given us. Grace is not something that can be earned! It is a gift.

Ephesians 2:5 Even when we were dead in sins, hath quickened us together with Christ, (by grace ye are saved;)

This scripture gives us a good description of how you cannot earn the grace of God because it was made available to us when we were still sinners.

Romans 5:8 But God commendeth his love toward us, in that, while we were yet sinners, Christ died for us.

1 John 2:2 And he is the propitiation for our sins: and not for ours only, but also for the sins of the whole world.

Jesus not only took your sins and my sins but the sins of the entire world were placed upon Him, past, present and future. All of our sin was paid for when Jesus went to the cross. So does that mean that everyone is automatically saved and we are all going to heaven? NO, even though salvation is a free gift of grace we must by faith receive that gift.

Ephesians 2:8 For by grace are ye saved through faith; and that not of yourselves: it is the gift of God.

Romans 5:1-2 Therefore being justified by faith, we have peace with God through our Lord Jesus Christ: By whom also we have access by faith into this grace wherein we stand, and rejoice in hope of the glory of God.

We need to understand that we must have both grace and faith working together so that we can receive all that God has provided for us. Ephesians 2:8 is a perfect example of how this works. You were not saved just because God decided one day that He was going to grant grace towards you and this was your day to be saved. Neither were you saved just because you worked so hard at being good. Grace is what God has made available to us because of the finished works that Jesus provided for us on the cross.

Some people have taught and are still teaching that the word grace is somehow describing the way in which God chooses to do things. They say God is in control of everything and God is only going to do what He wants to do and nothing ever happens unless God allows it to happen. If this is true then a lot of the people who are in prison for things like rape, murder and torture were only following God's will. That's completely wrong, that's not who God is and that's not His will. It's this same kind of thinking that says God puts sickness on people to try and teach them something. If you were to believe that God gave you a sickness or a disease and if you tried to get well by going to a doctor, taking medication or going to get prayed for by a healing ministry then you would be going against what you consider to be God's will.

The best way I can think of to describe grace would be to say that it is simply unearned favor from God.

WHAT IS FAITH?

Faith is what we must have in order for us to be able to receive the things that God has provided for us through grace. Every spiritual thing that you will ever need is already within your born again spirit. Faith is what will grab a hold of those things and bring them out from your spirit into your mind which is your soul and then into your body.

The fullness of Gods power is inside you in the form of the Holy Spirit. Remember I mentioned in chapter 2 that your mind is like a switch that turns on a pump that will flood your body with living water, which is the Holy Spirit.

Here is another way of looking at this: picture this power of God as a river of living water, it is an unlimited source that will never run dry. Now picture your mind as a big gate valve that controls the flow of this Spirit of living water. Your faith is what can open that valve, because your faith is directly linked to whatever you are focusing on. Faith is activated and stirred up by having positive thoughts about God and focusing on Jesus and the Holy Spirit wanting to work through you, and acknowledging every good thing He has placed in us which is Christ in us.

James 1:17 Every good gift and every perfect gift is from above, and cometh down from the Father of lights, with whom is no variableness, neither shadow of turning.

John 7:38 He that believeth on me, as the scripture hath said, out of his belly shall flow rivers of living water.

Hebrews 11:1 Now faith is the substance of things hoped for, the evidence of things not seen.

Faith is what produces the things that God has given us and makes them materialize. The things that you have been hoping for can become substance now. Faith is not something that is going to take place in the future; that is hope. Faith is action that takes place right now. It works by believing and not doubting what the word of God has promised us. Faith is being confident by trusting and knowing who you are in Christ.

Hebrews 11:6 But without faith it is impossible to please him: for he that cometh to God must believe that he is, and that he is a rewarder of them that diligently seek him.

So we now know that salvation is a free gift that has been offered to all of us by the grace of God and the only way we can receive this gift is through faith. We have to work at keeping ourselves in faith, but that is not works of the law.

Faith is our coming into agreement with what God has for us, it is our way of saying yes and amen to God believing that He wants us to have and use what He has given us. Works of the law is trying to get God to give us what He has already supplied for us by grace.

James 2:20 But wilt thou know, O vain man, that faith without works is dead?

Galatians 5:6 For in Jesus Christ neither circumcision availeth any thing, nor uncircumcision; but faith which worketh by love.

What these scriptures are teaching us is that it's going to take effort to maintain a life of faith. We are going to need to learn how to be in a place where we believe the word of God more than what people say. It's going to take work to be able to stay in faith and not be moved by all the things that are going on in the world. This is the same thing as we learned before about how you will have to labor to rest.

What would you do if a doctor tells you that there is something seriously wrong with you? Which report are you going to believe? Are you going to believe what the word of God says about healing? Or are you going to put your trust and faith in what the doctor says? If you begin to start putting more trust in what the doctor says than you have in the word of God, then you will shut off that gate valve which releases your faith. Faith has to be in operation in order for God's power to flow through you. A word of warning, you must know without a doubt that you are operating in faith before you decide to stop taking medication which your doctor has prescribed or if you decide to reject any treatment and medical procedures that your doctor has recommended. This can be dangerous because you cannot fake faith. If you are not absolutely sure then ask the Lord what He thinks you should do.

If you are still unsure then don't just <u>step out</u> in faith until you are convinced that you are <u>walking</u> in faith. Our faith is completely dependent upon the measure in which we believe. God will meet you were your faith is at. Faith is not something that we must reach out and grab a hold of from outside of us, it is something every born again believer already has and it's our job to learn how to use it.

> *Ephesians 3:20 Now unto him that is able to do exceeding abundantly above all that we ask or think, according to the power that worketh in us.*

This verse tells us how God is able to work through us and that the possibilities are more than we could ever imagine and that is what God's grace is.

However, the way this power works is according to how much we are willing to acknowledge and believe that we already possess all the fullness of that power within our spirit, this is what faith is. We have a part to play in working together with Christ and that is learning how to use our faith to release what God has placed in us by grace.

Fear, doubt and unbelief will close that valve and stop the power of God from working. Fear is completely opposite from faith and will actually produce negative results. Here is something to remember the letters F-E-A-R stand for **f**alse **e**vidence **a**ppearing **r**eal. We can grow to a point where our faith is unfailing when we enter into a place of rest, knowing that our faith cannot fail because of who we have become in Christ.

1 John 4:18 There is no fear in love; but perfect love casteth out fear: because fear hath torment. He that feareth is not made perfect in love.

Ephesians 3:16-19 That he would grant you, according to the riches of his glory, to be strengthened with might by his Spirit in the inner man; That Christ may dwell in your hearts by faith; that ye, being rooted and grounded in love, May be able to comprehend with all saints what is the breadth, and length, and depth, and height; And to know the love of Christ, which passeth knowledge, that ye might be filled with all the fulness of God.

The very essence of divine life is now in us because of faith. Just saying words is not enough they must be backed up by an activity of faith. You will never be able fight against the works of the devil until you realize that the power you now have inside you is much greater than any kind of demon and sickness there is. We must have such a bold confidence in our faith that we know we can actively defuse anything the devil tries to throw at us. This can only come by knowing that we already have the victory.

1 John 4:4 Ye are of God, little children, and have overcome them: because greater is he that is in you, than he that is in the world.

1 John 5:4 For whatsoever is born of God overcometh the world: and this is the victory that overcometh the world, even our faith.

Salvation is not the only thing we receive by grace through faith; you also receive forgiveness, healing, deliverance and prosperity. It all comes together as one package, and it was all provided as part of the finished works of the cross.

Like grace, faith has been abused and blown out of proportion to such an extreme that Gods grace is hardly recognized. We need to realize that there has to be equal amounts of both grace and faith so that we can properly work together with the Holy Spirit. If we start depending more on our faith and less of God's grace then we begin to fall away from the grace of God. If we were to only depend upon our faith to try and make something happen and fail to consider the grace God has given us, then that becomes works and works is of the law.

Romans 11:6 And if by grace, then is it no more of works: otherwise grace is no more grace. But if it be of works, then is it no more grace: otherwise work is no more work.

Romans 3:27 Where is boasting then? It is excluded. By what law? of works? Nay: but by the law of faith.

Romans 3:24-25 Being justified freely by his grace through the re-demption that is in Christ Jesus: Whom God hath set forth to be a propitiation through faith in his blood, to declare his righteousness for the remission of sins that are past, through the forbearance of God.

The word "works" is describing a legalistic way of trying to earn favor with God. Under the old covenant people had to work at trying to live a holy life according to the standard of laws which God had given them to live by. They were never able to keep all of these requirements or laws without failing in some part of it. If you were to fail in just one of these laws then you were in violation of the entire law. The only way to get back into right standing with God was through a priest. They were the only ones who were allowed to go behind the veil into the place called the Holy of Holies and be in God's presence. Only once a year were they allowed to make a sacrifice for the people's sins. The people of the Old Testament had to plead with God through prayer and fasting, they put on sack cloth and ashes to humble themselves. They needed to ask God to send His Holy Spirit down upon them when they required His help. Whenever the Holy Spirit came upon them to enable them He did not remain. He only stayed with them for as long as His service was needed. The old covenant was one of visitation; the new covenant is one of habitation.

There are many wonderful things which we can learn from studying the Old Testament it gives us great examples of what are both right and wrong ways to live. There is much to be gained by taking a look back into the history of how God related to people, and how people related to God. We would be short-changing ourselves if we were to never read and learn about the lives of the Old Testament saints and prophets. What we must understand is that they were living under a different covenant than we are and we need to study the Old Testament from a New Testament believer's perspective. Under the old covenant it was correct for them to pray the way they did because it was based on their performance.

Since we are no longer under the old covenant, we need to look at the fact that we are now under a covenant of grace and pray accordingly. One of the most common theories being taught today is that we are under an open heaven and that you have to try and pull things down from heaven. Most of what is mentioned throughout the Bible pertaining to an open heaven is referring to visions people have had. In the Old Testament and even in the gospels there are scriptures that talk about heaven being opened and the Holy Spirit coming down and resting upon people.

What people are failing to recognize is that after the day of Pentecost (Acts chapter two) those of us who are baptized in the Holy Spirit now have the full measure of Him abiding in us and He promises that He will never leave us. The presence of the Lord is always with us. When we are all gathered together during worship service He is in the midst of us because He is in us and we are releasing His presence. It's not because He just decided to show up there.

Romans 10:6 But the righteousness which is of faith speaketh on this wise, Say not in thine heart, Who shall ascend into heaven? (that is, to bring Christ down from above:)

Some people say things like Holy Spirit come and fill us, or Lord we ask you to come down and be with us, or Jesus come down and touch us and heal us.

When people pray this way then they have fallen from grace and have turned back to operating under the law. This comes from an old covenant mindset of trying to get God to do what He has already done. An open heaven is the life of Christ in us, all you need to do is let Him out.

Luke 17:20-21 And when he was demanded of the Pharisees, when the kingdom of God should come, he answered them and said, The kingdom of God cometh not with observation: Neither shall they say, Lo here! or, lo there! for, behold, the kingdom of God is within you.

Galatians 3:1-3 O foolish Galatians, who hath bewitched you, that ye should not obey the truth, before whose eyes Jesus Christ hath been evidently set forth, crucified among you? This only would I learn of you, Received ye the Spirit by the works of the law, or by the hearing of faith? Are ye so foolish? having begun in the Spirit, are ye now made perfect by the flesh?

Galatians 5:4 Christ is become of no effect unto you, whosoever of you are justified by the law; ye are fallen from grace.

Romans 3:20 Therefore by the deeds of the law there shall no flesh be justified in his sight: for by the law is the knowledge of sin.

Romans 6:14 For sin shall not have dominion over you: for ye are not under the law, but under grace.

So what has inspired people of today to pray from an old covenant mind set? Are they just doing what seems to be popular instead of considering what the word says? Have they forgotten that this covenant of grace is more than sufficient for us? Could it be that they are trying to mix the old covenant with the new covenant?

> *2 Corinthians 12:9 And he said unto me, My grace is sufficient for thee: for my strength is made perfect in weakness.*

> *Matthew 9:17 Neither do men put new wine into old bottles: else the bottles break, and the wine runneth out, and the bottles perish: but they put new wine into new bottles, and both are preserved.*

The old and the new covenant are like oil and water, we can't mix them together. You need to decide whether you want to live under the old covenant of law, or the new covenant of grace. There really should be no question about it when you consider the price Jesus has paid for us to live free from the law. It should be easy for us to say, "Yes by faith I believe."

> *Romans 3:28 Therefore we conclude that a man is justified by faith without the deeds of the law.*

CHAPTER 6

Heal the Sick

✤

So what is the most effective way to pray for the sick? My advice would be, don't. Jesus told us to go heal the sick, not to pray for them. Most of us are probably guilty of saying the same thing when someone comes to us for healing, and that is we always ask them, "Can I pray for you?" Although that may seem like a nice and polite thing to do, and we should always be polite and treat people with respect but it is actually incorrect because prayer will not produce healing, it only moves us into a place of receiving.

However my question is where did this idea come from that we are to pray for people that are in need of healing? Could it be that the church has somehow forgotten that Jesus came to establish a new and better way of doing things? The reason I bring this up is because these habits which the church has developed are pointing people in the wrong direction. This has become such a wide spread problem throughout the whole body of Christ that most of the time whenever I hear people minister healing to someone, they start praying and asking Jesus to come and heal this person. Has this become something that people just automatically say or are they saying what they believe?

In most cases people are just repeating something that they heard and then say to themselves if that person said this then that's how I should pray. I say that kind of thinking can steer you off course because how do you know if that person is actually right? Some people are operating in the supernatural gift that they have been given and if you try to copy them it may not work for you unless you also have that same gift.

We need to realize that God wants to use us and to work through us, but we limit Him through our lack of understanding of scripture and how God's kingdom works. There are rules and laws that God has established and we must find out what they are then learn how to obey and apply them to our lives because they will directly affect the amount of success we will have.

The first thing we need to know is that God obeys and follows His own laws and rules which He has established. There are both supernatural and natural laws and they all have a reason for being here. Sometimes we see them working together. Healing is a supernatural law that can manifest into the natural realm. How do we know this? It is because Jesus took all of our pain, sickness and disease upon Himself so we could be free of these things.

> *Isaiah 53:4-5 Surely he hath borne our griefs, and carried our sorrows: yet we did esteem him stricken, smitten of God, and afflicted. But he was wounded for our transgressions, he was bruised for our iniquities: the chastisement of our peace was upon him; and with his stripes we are healed.*

These two scriptures came from the prophet Isaiah hundreds of years before Jesus was born. There are hundreds of scriptures throughout the Old Testament that prophesied about

Jesus and we are able to find scriptures in the New Testament that reveal the fulfillment of those prophesies.

Matthew 8:16-17 When the even was come, they brought unto him many that were possessed with devils: and he cast out the spirits with his word, and healed all that were sick: That it might be fulfilled which was spoken by Esaias the prophet, saying, Himself took our infirmities, and bare our sicknesses.

1 Peter 2:24 Who his own self bare our sins in his own body on the tree, that we, being dead to sins, should live unto righteousness: by whose stripes ye were healed.

What we need to learn from studying these scriptures is that in the book of Isaiah we read that it says with His stripes we <u>are</u> healed. The reason it says we are healed is because it is talking about something that is going to take place in the future. Now in the New Testament 1 Peter 2:24 tells us that by whose stripes you <u>were</u> healed. This is describing something that has already happened! It's really important that we understand this because everything that has to do with healing is based on the fact that it's already been provided for us as part of the atonement; it is a finished work of the cross.

The day you got saved you received something that Jesus had obtained two thousand years ago when He went to the cross. He didn't come down here and shed His blood again just because you decided you needed to be saved one day. Healing works exactly the same way as salvation, in fact they both come together in the same package.

Under the new covenant a born again believer already has all the power they will ever need for healing all manners of sickness and disease. So if you need any type of healing don't expect Jesus to get up off His throne and come down here to heal you. Healing is an established law. You have Christ the healer living inside of you and He said I will never leave you. His final words on this were "It is finished."

Ephesians 1:18-20 The eyes of your understanding being enlightened; that ye may know what is the hope of his calling, and what the riches of the glory of his inheritance in the saints, And what is the exceeding greatness of his power to us-ward who believe, according to the working of his mighty power, Which he wrought in Christ, when he raised him from the dead, and set him at his own right hand in the heavenly places.

This power which worked in Christ when He was raised from the dead is God's power. It is the power of the Holy Spirit. This is the same power that has been granted to us. We have the same Holy Spirit in us that raised Jesus from the dead.

God wants us to understand that it is the hope of His calling that we will learn how to operate in this power; it is an inheritance for the saints. And what is the exceeding greatness of His power? It is much more powerful than we are able to comprehend and God has given it to us. Ephesians 1:20 is telling us that God has incorporated this mighty power in us. It is His gift to us. This scripture goes on to tell us that the way this power works is according to our belief which is our faith. Faith is another one of Gods laws which operates in both the supernatural and natural realm.

Romans 3:27 Where is boasting then? It is excluded. By what law? of works? Nay: but by the law of faith.

Since faith is one of Gods laws then we must learn how to use what God has given us and to cooperate with the way that God has set things up. There are different kinds of faith; there is a saving faith, which comes by hearing the word. You have to have faith in Jesus and what He has done before you can be saved and how would you even know about Jesus and the gift of salvation unless someone told you?

Once you are saved you now have the Spirit of Jesus living inside of you, this is your born again spirit and one of the fruits of the Spirit is faith.

Galatians 5:22-23 But the fruit of the Spirit is love, joy, peace, longsuffering, gentleness, goodness, faith, Meekness, temperance: against such there is no law.

There are nine gifts of the Spirit listed in 1 Corinthians chapter twelve. These gifts have been given to us by the Holy Spirit so He can work through us as needed for ministry, and one of those gifts is faith.

1 Corinthians 12:6-9 And there are diversities of operations, but it is the same God which worketh all in all. But the manifestation of the Spirit is given to every man to profit withal. For to one is given by the Spirit the word of wisdom; to another the word of knowledge by the same Spirit; To another faith by the same Spirit; to another the gifts of healing by the same Spirit.

2 Peter 1:1 Simon Peter, a servant and an apostle of Jesus Christ, to them that have obtained like precious faith with us through the righteousness of God and our Saviour Jesus Christ.

Like Peter we have obtained like precious faith because we have Jesus in us, we have His faith working in us. We don't need to pray and try to get God to give us more faith. We just need to trust and depend on the Holy Spirit to manifest forth the faith we already have in the Spirit. Sometimes the Holy Spirit will stir us up, and He may point someone out to you, when this happens we can be so moved with compassion that we will have an overwhelming desire to see that person healed. At other times we need to stir ourselves up to be able to position ourselves into a place of operating in faith. This is why faith is a law of operation because nothing will happen until your faith has been activated and then released.

When we are using the like precious faith which is the faith of Christ in us, then it becomes a supernaturally enhanced form of faith, it enables us to believe for something like healing.

The reason faith is a law of operation is because it requires us to act and do something. We must make a decision that we are going to believe. We know that faith is in us and that it can bring forth things like healing, if we can let it out. First stir yourself up, by worship, prayer or whatever works best for you. Say to the Holy Spirit, "I stir you up in me." It's as simple as flipping a switch. Picture in your mind a light switch now picture yourself turning on that switch and releasing His presence.

James 2:26 For as the body without the spirit is dead, so faith without works is dead also.

Romans 12:3 For I say, through the grace given unto me, to every man that is among you, not to think of himself more highly than he ought to think; but to think soberly, according as God hath dealt to every man the measure of faith.

Everyone who is born again has been given <u>the</u> same measure of faith and it is the same measure of faith that was able to raise Jesus from the dead.

Jesus is our perfect example of how healing works. We need to follow His instructions and see ourselves doing what He did. Jesus healed multitudes of people and there is nowhere in scripture that says He prayed for their healing. The only thing that comes close to this is when Jesus raised Lazarus from the dead. The reason Jesus prayed this time was because He had to keep coming against the negative things that these people were speaking forth, He had to keep telling them to believe.

John 11:41-42 Then they took away the stone from the place where the dead was laid. And Jesus lifted up his eyes, and said, Father, I thank thee that thou hast heard me. And I knew that thou hearest me always: but because of the people which stand by I said It, that they may believe that thou hast sent me.

John 11:21-23 Then said Martha unto Jesus, Lord, if thou hadst been here, my brother had not died. But I know, that even now, whatsoever thou wilt ask of God, God will give it thee. Jesus saith unto her, Thy brother shall rise again.

John 11:37 And some of them said, Could not this man, which opened the eyes of the blind, have caused that even this man should not have died?

Even the doubt and unbelief that is created by the people around us can severely hinder or stop a person from receiving the manifestation of healing power that someone is releasing. Jesus had to raise the faith in the people around him in order to counteract their unbelief. This event of raising Lazarus from the dead is not the only time in scripture where we see that Jesus had to first deal with the unbelief that was coming from the people around Him before He could see a miracle happen. It is not that this atmosphere of unbelief was able to somehow limit the flow of power that Jesus had, but rather it is what can diminish or even destroy the faith of those who need to receive.

We see another place in scripture where Jesus had to get all of the doubting unbelievers out of the house before He could raise the ruler's daughter from the dead.

Mark 5:38-42 And he cometh to the house of the ruler of the synagogue, and seeth the tumult, and them that wept and wailed greatly. And when he was come in, he saith unto them, Why make ye this ado, and weep? the damsel is not dead, but sleepeth. And they laughed him to scorn. But when he had put them all out, he taketh the father and the mother of the damsel, and them that were with him, and entereth in where the damsel was lying. And he took the damsel by the hand, and said unto her, Talitha cumi; which is, being interpreted, Damsel, I say unto thee, arise. And straightway the damsel arose, and walked; for she was of the age of twelve years. And they were astonished with a great astonishment.

Here is another incident where a blind man needed healing but the town where this man lived was so filled with unbelievers that Jesus had to take the man out of that town before the man could receive his healing.

Mark 8:23-26 And he took the blind man by the hand, and led him out of the town; and when he had spit on his eyes, and put his hands upon him, he asked him if he saw ought. And he looked up, and said, I see men as trees, walking. After that he put his hands again upon his eyes, and made him look up: and he was restored, and saw every man clearly. And he sent him away to his house, saying, Neither go into the town, nor tell it to any in the town.

Why is it that this is the only place in scripture where we see that Jesus had to lay His hands on someone a second time? It was because this man had been around so much unbelief that even though Jesus had taken this man out of that unbelieving town, the man still had a certain amount of unbelief left in him.

Notice that Jesus told this man not to go back into that town or to tell anyone that he had received his sight. The reason for that is because when people start saying negative things in unbelief it can cause someone to lose their healing. We always need to be aware of the fact that people can plant bad seed in us without us even knowing that this is happening. We must always guard ourselves from receiving bad seed.

Matthew 13:54-58 And when he was come into his own country, he taught them in their synagogue, insomuch that they were astonished, and said, Whence hath this man this wisdom, and these mighty works? Is not this the carpenter's son? is not his mother called Mary? and his brethren, James, and Joses, and Simon, and Judas? And his sisters, are they not all with us? Whence then hath this man all these things? And they were offended in him. But Jesus said unto them, A prophet is not without honour, save in his own country, and in his own house. And he did not many mighty works there because of their unbelief.

Again we see here in the scripture above another example of how unbelief can hinder us from receiving what God wants us to have. The people who lived in the town where Jesus had grown up only knew Him as a man and were not able to recognize Him for who He truly was, both man and God manifested in the flesh.

So how can we overcome this unbelief? First we need to understand that there are three different types of unbelief. There is an unbelief that comes from not knowing or understanding who Jesus really is. The next type of unbelief comes from wrong teaching, such as healing and miracles were only for the apostles, it's not for us now. Both of these types of unbelief can be corrected by teaching people the truth. The last type of unbelief is a natural unbelief; it comes from your natural senses.

When you are paying more attention to how your body feels instead of what you know to be true according to scripture, then unbelief can set in. It may be a fact that you feel sick or have pain in your body but the truth says by His stripes you <u>were</u> healed (1 Peter 2:24). The truth is always greater and more real than fact. Are you going to believe God's word for healing or are you going to let your feelings decide for you? We need to stand strong believing what we know is true because healing can sometimes take a while to manifest in our physical body, while at the same time someone else is instantly healed. If you are having problems receiving healing it could be because of this natural form of unbelief and the only way to get rid of this natural unbelief is through prayer and fasting.

A man brought his son to the disciples because the boy needed deliverance from a demonic spirit. The man told them that this spirit takes hold of the boy and makes him lunatic and will throw him into the fire or into the water. This man told Jesus that he had brought the boy to the disciples but they could not cure him.

Matthew 17:18-21 And Jesus rebuked the devil; and he departed out of him: and the child was cured from that very hour. Then came the disciples to Jesus apart, and said, Why could not we cast him out? And Jesus said unto them, Because of your unbelief: for verily I say unto you, If ye have faith as a grain of mustard seed, ye shall say unto this mountain, Remove hence to yonder place; and it shall remove; and nothing shall be impossible unto you. Howbeit this kind goeth not out but by prayer and fasting.

Jesus is telling His disciples how to get rid of this kind of unbelief not a certain kind of demon. All demons are under the authority of the name of Jesus. If you think that they are going to leave because you went on a hunger strike then you are going to have some major problems. Neither can you cast them out by praying. These scriptures are telling us how to overcome unbelief. Your body which is referred to as the flesh is what most people listen to. They depend on their body to tell them how they feel and what they need. We need to reprogram our minds to the truth that we are a brand new creation and the flesh is no longer in charge. Fasting will not cause God to move and do something it will only move us. The reason the Bible tells us to both fast and pray is because when we fast we are denying our flesh, our carnal side and are seeking God and drawing near to Him. If we aren't seeking God through prayer while we fast, it becomes nothing more than a hunger strike.

Refusing to forgive someone can also hinder us from receiving from God. If you are mad at someone then you need to forgive them. If somebody has done something to you in the past and you are still angry with them then that anger can cause you problems and you need to learn how to forgive them. God forgave us because He loves us and He expects us to look at people from a place of love and not anger. When you forgive someone then you need to mean it, this does not mean that you can go back and pick up that anger again. Once you forgive someone that should be the end of it. If for some reason you are having trouble with this then ask the Holy Spirit to help you. Don't go back into the past and try to recall every incident where you got mad at someone, you will know if you are still mad at them or not. The Lord does not want us to live in the past. He has forgotten your past and you need to do the same. Jesus and the Holy Spirit are there for you, so if you are still having a hard time forgiving someone then turn your cares over to Jesus.

1 Peter 5: 7 Casting all your care upon him, for he careth for you.

Luke 6:37 Judge not, and ye shall not be judged: condemn not, and ye shall not be condemned: forgive, and ye shall be forgiven:

Matthew 18:21-22 Then came Peter to him, and said, Lord, how oft shall my brother sin against me, and I forgive him? till seven times? Jesus saith unto him, I say not unto thee, Until seven times: but, Until seventy times seven.

Matthew 11:28 Come unto me, all ye that labour and are heavy laden, and I will give you rest.

Another thing that can limit us from receiving and seeing Gods power flow through us is pride. People who think that they can do everything themselves are operating in pride because they have exalted themselves and are not depending on God. Pride is not just having an arrogant attitude it is also when people have a low opinion about themselves because they are still focusing on themselves. Being self centered and putting ourselves first has become a normal way of life these days but it is going against what Gods word says.

James 4:6 But he giveth more grace. Wherefore he saith, God resisteth the proud, but giveth grace unto the humble.

1 Peter 5:5-6 Likewise, ye younger, submit yourselves unto the elder. Yea, all of you be subject one to another, and be clothed with humility: for God resisteth the proud, and giveth grace to the humble. Humble yourselves therefore under the mighty hand of God, that he may exalt you in due time.

Proverbs 29:23 A man's pride shall bring him low: but honour shall uphold the humble in spirit.

Matthew 23:12 And whosoever shall exalt himself shall be abased; and he that shall humble himself shall be exalted.

Proverbs 16:18-19 Pride goeth before destruction, and an haughty spirit before a fall. Better it is to be of an humble spirit with the lowly, than to divide the spoil with the proud.

There are so many scriptures that that teach us about the downfalls of pride, and the advantages of being humble that I don't have room enough in this chapter to list them all, you need to look these up for yourself.

Why is God so displeased with pride? It's because pride comes from the devil. Pride is what caused Lucifer to think that he might be able to elevate himself to a position that was equal to God.

Isaiah 14:12-14 How art thou fallen from heaven, O Lucifer, son of the morning! how art thou cut down to the ground, which didst weaken the nations! For thou hast said in thine heart, I will ascend into heaven, I will exalt my throne above the stars of God: I will sit also upon the mount of the congregation, in the sides of the north: I will ascend above the heights of the clouds; I will be like the most High.

A MORE EFFECTIVE WAY TO PRAY

Praying is simply talking to God. There are methods in which we can pray that will produce more effective results. Healing is a perfect example of how this works. When people come to us for healing we first ask God what He wants to say to them. He almost always gives me a word or two for that person. There have been times when He has given me more than a few words and times when I did not get anything at first but after we started ministering to them then I would get something. We always ask people what they would like prayer for and that's helpful because it shows us where their faith is at and what they are believing for.

However, it is always better to first ask God what someone needs because some people don't even know what it is that they need. This is where you really need to hear from God. I will ask Him how He wants to minister to that person because sometimes there are things going on in someone's life that have to be dealt with and it might take time to get that person into a place where they can be set free. There have been times when we had to first break off hindrances before we could minister to them. Praying for someone's healing should really be asking God to reveal to us if there is anything that maybe blocking that person from receiving their healing. We are not trying to get God to heal them; we are trying to raise that person's faith into a place where they are able to receive the healing that already has been provided for them.

John 8:32 And ye shall know the truth, and the truth shall make you free.

Whatever kind of physical condition that someone is suffering with is no big deal because every type of sickness and disease is under the feet of Jesus. Once we get someone into a place of believing the truth then healing is easy. Ask the person you are ministering to if it's ok if you lay your hands on them, usually on their shoulder or the top of their head, don't just put your hands on them wherever they have a problem unless they say it's ok to do so.

Then take your authority over that condition and speak to it. Command it to leave in the name of Jesus. If the person you are ministering to did not receive then keep ministering to them until they understand that healing is something they already have as part of the atonement. It's ok to speak to someone's pain level and to release the anointing power again. However, we should only command a sickness or disease to leave one time. Teach them how to stand in faith knowing that they are healed even if they don't feel it. We must first believe before we see the manifestation of that healing.

If you are ministering healing to yourself and you speak forth a command, believe it, stand firm on it believing that your words have power in them. If you think that you need to keep repeating the same command over this condition then you did not believe the words that you spoke the first time. You were operating in unbelief and that will stop the flow of Gods power. Stand firm believing your first command. If you are not seeing the manifestation of whatever you have commanded then speak to your body telling it to receive what you have previously spoken. You can also break off anything that may be hindering you. If you feel like you need to do more, try praying in the Spirit. These are just some examples. You really need to follow the leading of the Holy Spirit because each one of us is going to have a different need. Remember that Jesus is always our perfect example to follow not some method of praying that you may have learned in church.

> *Acts 10:38 How God anointed Jesus of Nazareth with the Holy Ghost and with power: who went about doing good, and healing all that were oppressed of the devil; for God was with him.*

God does not want you to be sick or in pain it is always Gods will for you to be healed. The reason that not everyone receives healing is not because God's refusing to heal them, it's because their faith has been diluted with doubt and unbelief. You have the same Holy Spirit that God anointed Jesus with, it is the same amount of power, the only difference is that Jesus had no doubt or unbelief.

> *Luke 5:12-13 And it came to pass, when he was in a certain city, behold a man full of leprosy: who seeing Jesus fell on his face, and besought him, saying, Lord, if thou wilt, thou canst make me clean. And he put forth his hand, and touched him, saying, I will: be thou clean. And immediately the leprosy departed from him.*

When the man who was full of leprosy came to Jesus and asked Jesus if it was His will that he be healed, Jesus said yes and

He healed the man. This man had every right to ask that question because the time he was living in was before the cross.

The new covenant did not come into effect until after Jesus had gone to the cross. Under the new covenant you would be asking in unbelief if it's His will to heal, because it's part of the finished works of the cross. We should all know that His answer is always, "Yes of course it's my will."

Matthew 10:1 And when he had called unto him his twelve disciples, he gave them power against unclean spirits, to cast them out, and to heal all manner of sickness and all manner of disease.

Mark 6:12-13 And they went out, and preached that men should repent. And they cast out many devils, and anointed with oil many that were sick, and healed them.

Mark 3:14-15 And he ordained twelve, that they should be with him, and that he might send them forth to preach, And to have power to heal sicknesses, and to cast out devils.

Notice that when Jesus ordained and sent forth His disciples He told them to heal the sick, cast out unclean spirits and to raise the dead. He never told them to pray and ask God to do this for them. We see in the gospels that there were so many people that were coming to Jesus and His disciples for healing and deliverance that Jesus had to send even more people out to help meet the needs of all who were oppressed.

Luke 10:1-2 After these things the Lord appointed other seventy also, and sent them two and two before his face into every city and place, whither he himself would come. Therefore said he unto them, The harvest truly is great, but the labourers are few: pray ye therefore the Lord of the harvest, that he would send forth labourers into his harvest.

Luke 10:17 And the seventy returned again with joy, saying, Lord, even the devils are subject unto us through thy name.

Luke 10:9 And heal the sick that are therein, and say unto them, The kingdom of God is come nigh unto you.

We as New Testament believers have also been ordained to operate as citizens of God's heavenly kingdom. We have been given power and authority over all manners of sickness and disease. We also have been given power and authority to cast out devils and every kind of unclean spirit in Jesus name.

2 Corinthians 3:6 Who also hath made us able ministers of the new testament; not of the letter, but of the spirit: for the letter killeth, but the spirit giveth life.

Luke 10:19 Behold, I give unto you power to tread on serpents and scorpions, and over all the power of the enemy: and nothing shall by any means hurt you.

SPEAK TO YOUR MOUNTAIN

Mark 11:23 For verily I say unto you, That whosoever shall say unto this mountain, Be thou removed, and be thou cast into the sea; and shall not doubt in his heart, but shall believe that those things which he saith shall come to pass; he shall have whatsoever he saith.

Jesus is telling us that a mountain can be some kind of an obstacle that is standing in our way. Sickness or disease can become one of those obstacles. Jesus uses a mountain to describe something big that could be impossible for us to move without having help from God. It is true that we can do nothing on our own but we can do all things through Christ who is in us.

John 15:5 I am the vine, ye are the branches: He that abideth in me, and I in him, the same bringeth forth much fruit: for without me ye can do nothing.

Philippians 4:13 I can do all things through Christ which strengtheneth me.

Jesus is telling us that we need to take our authority based on who we are in Christ and speak out loud directly to whatever kind of sickness or disease we may have and command it to leave in His name. He is also telling us that we don't need faith that's any bigger than a mustard seed in order to see these things removed.

Although we need to have our faith working before we can see the evidence of healing, we don't need to use a huge amount of faith. What we need is to get rid of any doubt or unbelief. This also applies if you are going to lay hands on someone for healing. Not only do we need to be operating in faith so that we can release His power from within us, but the person who is being ministered to has to have enough faith to believe and receive.

Mark 11:12-14 And on the morrow, when they were come from Bethany, he was hungry: And seeing a fig tree afar off having leaves, he came, if haply he might find any thing thereon: and when he came to it, he found nothing but leaves; for the time of figs was not yet. And Jesus answered and said unto it, No man eat fruit of thee hereafter for ever. And his disciples heard it.

Mark 11:20-21 And in the morning, as they passed by, they saw the fig tree dried up from the roots. And Peter calling to remembrance saith unto him, Master, behold, the fig tree which thou cursedst is withered away.

Matthew 21:21-22 Jesus answered and said unto them, Verily I say unto you, If ye have faith, and doubt not, ye shall not only do this which is done to the fig tree, but also if ye shall say unto this mountain, Be thou removed, and be thou cast into the sea; it shall be done. And all things, whatsoever ye shall ask in prayer, believing, ye shall receive.

Praying should be mostly about thanking and praising God instead of begging and pleading and continually asking God to do something for you like some ungrateful greedy little snot nosed kid. Jesus told us that God is not like some unjust judge that you have to keep pestering if you want an answer from Him.

Luke 18:1 And he spake a parable unto them to this end, that men ought always to pray, and not to faint.

What Jesus is telling us here when He says, "and to not faint," is that we should not completely give up and never pray to God again just because you thought your prayer did not get answered. This parable will explain how God will answer your prayer quickly if you read the whole thing.

Luke 18:7-8 And shall not God avenge his own elect, which cry day and night unto him, though he bear long with them? I tell you that he will avenge them speedily. Nevertheless when the Son of man cometh, shall he find faith on the earth?

We need to remember that when we pray we are talking to God! You may want to think about what it is that you are going to say to Him before you just start firing words out at Him like a machine gun. You probably are going to hear a lot more from God if you approach Him as a friend. God wants us to depend on Him for instruction and He loves to talk with us and answer our questions, however we just need to use a little common sense.

Sickness and disease are demonic and healing has to come from us using the authority we now have as believers, not by praying and asking Jesus to come and do this for us. He has raised us up to be mighty warriors that have been given power and authority over satan and all demons. Things like cancer come from a demonic spirit and that has to be cast out. People are not going to be set free of something like cancer just because we love them. This is not to say that we don't love people. We need to love people as Jesus did and want to see people set free of sickness and demonic oppression, this is the reason why we cast demons out!

1 Corinthians 13:1 Though I speak with the tongues of men and of angels, and have not charity, I am become as sounding brass, or a tinkling cymbal.

Matthew 10:7-8 And as ye go, preach, saying, The kingdom of heaven is at hand. Heal the sick, cleanse the lepers, raise the dead, cast out devils: freely ye have received, freely give.

Matthew 8:16 When the even was come, they brought unto him many that were possessed with devils: and he cast out the spirits with his word, and healed all that were sick.

Notice that Jesus had to use His words to cast out these demons. They didn't just leave because His presence was there. If Jesus needed to tell these demons to come out then we certainly do to.

If you are ministering to someone that has cancer then you need to tell them that the root cause or source of that cancer comes from a demonic spirit and that spirit has to be cast out. You need to be up front with them and tell them what's going on and let them decide if they want to be set free. Ask them if they are a born again Christian because they will need the authority of Jesus to remain free. Lay hands on them and take your authority and tell these demons to leave that person in Jesus name.

Speak to that cancer and command it to die in Jesus name. Speak life into the place where that cancer was and release the presence of the Holy Spirit into them. Things like Aids, addictions, arthritis, autism, cancers, chronic fatigue syndrome, depression, epilepsy and fibromyalgia, these are just a few of the many things that come from a demonic source and need to be dealt with as the spiritual cause behind them.

If I start to feel any kind of sickness coming on me I speak to it and I reject it in the name of Jesus before it has a chance to develop. If a doctor tries to tell me I have something wrong with me I immediately say, " I reject that in Jesus name." I don't care what the doctor thinks or if he agrees with me or not because I have learned that this is how I can stop something before it becomes a problem. When we hear things on TV that start talking about sickness we say I reject that in Jesus name. I no longer believe in getting sick and neither my wife nor I have been sick in years. Once sickness has had a chance to become established in you then it is much harder to get rid of. It would have been better if it was dealt with from the start. Sickness and disease are no match compared to the name of Jesus and it must obey someone who is operating under the authority of Jesus.

Try speaking to your problems and see what happens. Speak to pain. Say, "I command all pain to leave in Jesus name." Or, "headache be gone in Jesus name." Thank God and give Him all the glory for working through you.

People need to be made aware that things like sin, hate, anger, refusing to forgive someone and even pride can provide a way for satan to attack us. When ministering to people let the Holy Spirit reveal these things to you before you proceed, because if we try to assume the role of being a psychologist were going to make a mess of things.

> *John 14:12 Verily, verily, I say unto you, He that believeth on me, the works that I do shall he do also; and greater works than these shall he do; because I go unto my Father.*

This business of praying and asking God to heal us or someone else is an old covenant way of doing things and it was perfectly fine for people in the Old Testament to ask God for healing but we are no longer under the old covenant. Under the new covenant Jesus tells us to take our authority and speak to our problems. Your body is voice activated because that is how God created you in the first place. Your body is going to respond to the words of our creator. Words form pictures on the inside of you. When you are ministering the truth (which is the word) to someone, it paints a positive picture for them of how they see or think of themselves. We all need to have a positive image of ourselves being well and prosperous. The word of God will paint an image in our mind of how God sees us and how He wants us to see ourselves.

Jeremiah 29:11 For I know the thoughts that I think toward you, saith the LORD, thoughts of peace, and not of evil, to give you an expected end.

3 John 2 Beloved, I wish above all things that thou mayest prosper and be in health, even as thy soul prospereth.

CHAPTER 7

Our Crumbling and Declining Nation

⚜

LOOKING BACK THROUGH HISTORY AT the time when our country was first formed into a governmental system and considering the amount of thought and ethics involved in this process, it is truly amazing what the founders of our country were able to establish as a working order in which we are able to successfully live and thrive as a nation. Not only did the system in which they designed work well but America became the strongest and most prosperous nation.

Where did the founding fathers of our nation come up with such great wisdom to be able to write all these things that work so well? They used the Bible as a guide and instruction manual as a foundation on how to structure such a system. Not only is there evidence of scripture being used throughout the writing of the Constitution but there are documented letters stating that the people who were designated to working on the formation of this Constitution and amendments would first pray and ask for wisdom and guidance. There are also documented cases that state where the entire designated staff would attend a church service before they started working. There were also some other letters that stated that the church was used as a meeting hall that these people could work in after they had prayed and spent time in the scriptures.

Our country was founded on biblical principles and the Bible became the educational textbook for teaching people how to read. Even some of the people that were involved in government who claimed not to be Christians were still known to have quoted the Bible because they were taught to use these moral principles as a guide line in which they could live by.

The following is a quote from Benjamin Franklin, signer of the Constitution and Declaration of Independence.

I have lived, Sir, a long time, and the longer I live, the more convincing proofs I see of this truth, that God governs in the affairs of men. And if a sparrow cannot fall to the ground without His notice, is it probable that an empire can rise without his aid? We have been assured, Sir, in the Sacred Writings, that "except the Lord build the House, they labor in vain that build it." I firmly believe this; and I also believe that without His concurring aid we shall succeed in this political building no better, than the Builders of Babel: We shall be divided by our partial local interests; our projects will be confounded, and we ourselves shall become a reproach and bye word down to future ages. And what is worse, mankind may hereafter from this unfortunate instance, despair of establishing governments by human wisdom and leave it to chance, war and conquest.

I therefore beg leave to move that henceforth prayers imploring the assistance of Heaven, and its blessings on our deliberations be held in this Assembly every morning before we proceed to business, and that one or more of the clergy of this city be requested to officiate in that service.

(Source: James Madison, The Records of the Federal Convention of 1787, Max Farrand, editor (New Haven: Yale University Press, 1911), Vol. I, pp. 450-452, June 28, 1787.)

The following two quotes are from John Quincy Adams, sixth president of the United States:

The law given from Sinai was a civil and municipal as well as a moral and religious code; it contained many statutes…of universal application-laws essential to the existence of men in society, and most of which have been enacted by every nation which ever professed any code of laws.

(Source: John Quincy Adams, Letters of John Quincy Adams, to His Son, on the Bible and Its Teachings (Auburn: James M. Alden, 1850), p. 61.)

There are three points of doctrine the belief of which forms the foundation of all morality. The first is the existence of God; the second is the immortality of the human soul; and the third is a future state of rewards and punishments. Suppose it possible for a man to disbelieve either of these three articles of faith and that man will have no conscience, he will have no other law than that of the tiger or the shark. The laws of man may bind him in chains or may put him to death, but they never can make him wise, virtuous, or happy.

(Source: John Quincy Adams, Letters of John Quincy Adams to His Son on the Bible and Its Teachings (Auburn: James M. Alden, 1850), pp. 22-23.)

These letters and documents that were written which make up our Constitution and amendments are not some secret that is being withheld from us, they are of public record and you have a right to read them. It would almost seem as though these things have been forgotten and everyone is just putting their trust in what the government officials are telling them. I can't help but wonder if some of these elected government officials even know what some of these original documents say, or if they even care what they say, after all they may have an agenda that might seem more important to them than what the Bible says because they are more interested in adjusting their morals to fit the time we now live in.

If our founding fathers could somehow see the state of our nation today I am sure they would not be pleased. They would certainly know that something has gone wrong.

Why is it that we as a nation can't seem to learn something by looking back at our own past? Sure we are living in a different time but does that mean that we should compromise our ethical standards? Certainly we should not have compromised and this is not something that just happened over night but rather it is something that slowly started to change and take place over a long period of time.

Jeremiah 5:25-26 Your iniquities have turned away these things, and your sins have withholden good things from you. For among my people are found wicked men: they lay wait, as he that setteth snares; they set a trap, they catch men.

We have been taught that our nation was founded as a nation under God, and it is even printed on our money, In God We Trust. God's word is what tells us how a governmental system should be constructed and which laws must be in place for it to function properly. There are many examples of this throughout the Bible that would indicate what type of governmental systems were successful and which ones failed.

Psalms 9:17 The wicked shall be turned into hell, and all the nations that forget God.

Proverbs 14:34 Righteousness exalteth a nation: but sin is a reproach to any people.

Jeremiah 7:28 But thou shalt say unto them, This is a nation that obeyeth not the voice of the LORD their God, nor receiveth correction: truth is perished, and is cut off from their mouth.

Our founding fathers of this nation had enough sense to depend on God and His word for advice instead of trying to create something on their own. We would be wise to follow their example if we want to see this country turn around and be more successful. America truly is a great nation because it started out trusting and depending on God and because of that devotion God has blessed this nation and still is blessing us.

God is not judging this country; neither is He pouring out His wrath upon our country because of the mistakes we have made. We as a nation are experiencing the consequences of the sins we are committing and this is what has given satan an opportunity to cause problems throughout our society. Have we forgotten where our help comes from?

Romans 13:13-14 Let us walk honestly, as in the day; not in rioting and drunkenness, not in chambering and wantonness, not in strife and envying. But put ye on the Lord Jesus Christ, and make not provision for the flesh, to fulfil the lusts thereof.

John 5:22 For the Father judgeth no man, but hath committed all judgment unto the Son.

Isaiah 65:1-2 I am sought of them that asked not for me; I am found of them that sought me not: I said, Behold me, behold me, unto a nation that was not called by my name. I have spread out my hands all the day unto a rebellious people, which walketh in a way that was not good, after their own thoughts.

As we look back through the history of the Bible we always find that the nations which were successful were the ones that were seeking God.

The Kings of those nations were working together with the priest and the prophets. The church has always had a major part to play towards influencing and offering advice to help the government function. The church also provided unity, support and spiritual strength to the people. Something has changed in our country. The government seems to be turning away from the church and is no longer seeking the advice of the church. Could this be because they first stopped using the Bible in schools and replaced them with academic text books? Could it be that the people who are running for political office have had little or no Christian influence in their lives? Would this somehow explain the reason why we no longer see a biblical influence in our government offices? Could it be that the church has lost its voice and the government no longer seems to be listening to the church or turning to them for advice?

Is it possible that this lack of church influence could be having a negative effect on society? After all the government should be setting an example for us to follow. Has the church lost its confidence and shut themselves up inside their buildings where they won't bother anybody? Could it be that the church might be afraid of what people are going to say about them if they start voicing their opinion?

The church should be making much more of a difference and having a greater impact on society than they are. I'm not saying that all churches are not doing their part there are some great churches that really are making a difference now and I believe that they are starting to make an impact on other churches as well; the problem is that the majority of churches in this country are not willing to make any kind of change. They seem to be stuck in the way that they have chosen to do things and are relying more upon their religious traditions and handed down doctrines than they are on what the Bible says.

Colossians 2:8 Beware lest any man spoil you through philosophy and vain deceit, after the tradition of men, after the rudiments of the world, and not after Christ.

No wonder the government has backed off from listening to the church. Most of these churches can't even seem to agree with each other because they have all formed their own separate opinion and really aren't paying much attention to what the Bible says. They are so afraid that they might offend someone that they are willing to compromise their messages by only picking out certain passages of scripture that they know won't rub anyone the wrong way. Some churches are mostly relying on teachings that other people have made and sermons that they get off of the internet.

It would appear that the government and the church have both gone their separate ways and are working independent of each other. There are certain groups of people in our nation that are becoming more bold when it comes to demanding that some ungodly changes should be made and the government is backing up those things and passing laws that should have never been passed. While a large portion of the church has become more withdrawn and is not taking a stand against all the immoral and corrupt things that are being allowed these days.

Our nation has changed course from where it once started out and is now headed in a totally different ethical direction. Has our country become more influenced by big businesses that can produce a lot of money?

Have we compromised what is considered to be right and settled for justifying things that maybe wrong just because they make money? The Bible tells us that in the last days we will see these kinds of changes taking place in our society.

2 Timothy 3:1-5 This know also, that in the last days perilous times shall come. For men shall be lovers of their own selves, covetous, boasters, proud, blasphemers, disobedient to parents, unthankful, unholy, Without natural affection, trucebreakers, false accusers, incontinent, fierce, despisers of those that are good, Traitors, heady, highminded, lovers of pleasures more than lovers of God; Having a form of godliness, but denying the power thereof: from such turn away.

These scriptures we see in second Timothy chapter 3 is a Bible prophesy that is now taking place in our society and it is happening because mankind is not capable of running a country and its government without relying on God's instruction and moral laws. Whenever a nation has tried to do things on their own, independent of God, the end result has always been destruction.

Isaiah 1:4 Ah sinful nation, a people laden with iniquity, a seed of evildoers, children that are corrupters: they have forsaken the LORD, they have provoked the Holy One of Israel unto anger, they are gone away backward.

The devil is taking advantage of the fact that we as a nation have been turning away from the word of God and he is fueling the thoughts of people who produce movies, video games and other related things. Even sermons that are being preached in some of the churches today are being mixed with stuff that is not in the Bible. Satan will do whatever he can to try and interfere with a message that is coming from the word of God.

Matthew 24:24 For there shall arise false Christs, and false prophets, and shall shew great signs and wonders; insomuch that, if it were possible, they shall deceive the very elect.

2 Peter 2:1-2 But there were false prophets also among the people, even as there shall be false teachers among you, who privily shall bring in damnable heresies, even denying the Lord that bought them, and bring upon themselves swift destruction. And many shall follow their pernicious ways; by reason of whom the way of truth shall be evil spoken of.

2 Timothy 4:3-4 For the time will come when they will not endure sound doctrine; but after their own lusts shall they heap to

themselves teachers, having itching ears; And they shall turn away
their ears from the truth, and shall be turned unto fables.

It is extremely important for us to know what the word of
God says so we won't fall into this kind of deception. You will
never be able to notice what a wrong teaching is if you don't know
what the truth is. There is no teaching outside of the Bible that
you can benefit more from. There is far more for you to learn
from the Bible than you could ever learn in a life time. The
Holy Spirit will help you to better understand what the scriptures
mean. He is not going to teach you things that are outside of the
Bible. We need to stay within the word and let the Holy Spirit
teach us even if we think we know what the word says because He
is in us and in Him is the mind of Christ.

1 John 2:20 But ye have an unction from the Holy One, and ye
know all things.

1John 2:27 But the anointing which ye have received of him abi-
deth in you, and ye need not that any man teach you: but as the
same anointing teacheth you of all things, and is truth, and is no lie,
and even as it hath taught you, ye shall abide in him.

We need to get to a place where we no longer have to depend on the pastor of a church to spoon feed the word to us.
We will never grow spiritually if we become complacent in this
sort of way. When we depend on someone else to teach us we
are subjecting ourselves to seeing things from their point of view
instead of getting our own revelation from God about what these
scriptures are telling us. There can be many things which are
revealed in just one passage of scripture, but there is only one

truth which can be found from studying that passage of scripture. Another way of saying this would be that a scripture does not have more than one theological meaning to it. Just because many people may understand it in different ways does not mean that they are all correct.

Hebrews 5:12-14 For when for the time ye ought to be teachers, ye have need that one teach you again which be the first principles of the oracles of God; and are become such as have need of milk, and not of strong meat. For every one that useth milk is unskilful in the word of righteousness: for he is a babe. But strong meat belongeth to them that are of full age, even those who by reason of use have their senses exercised to discern both good and evil.

The Holy Spirit has to have something He can use. You need to know the truth and to have that word of truth established in you so that the things you are learning will be able to bear witness with the Holy Spirit who now lives in your spirit.

John 14:26 But the Comforter, which is the Holy Ghost, whom the Father will send in my name, he shall teach you all things, and bring all things to your remembrance, whatsoever I have said unto you.

John 1:1 In the beginning was the Word, and the Word was with God, and the Word was God.

Hebrews 10:7 Then said I, Lo, I come (in the volume of the book it is written of me,) to do thy will, O God.

Jesus is the Word of God. The words He speaks to you are the truth and this is what the Holy Spirit will reveal to you. Jesus can speak to you through your spirit and He also speaks to us through scriptures. There should never be any variation or deviation that is allowed to lead us away from this truth. God is not going to come up with something new for us; we have not yet even come close to discovering what the Bible has for us. The Bible was given to us so we can learn and it is also something that we can use as a reference guide to determine whether something is true or false.

I am not against the church, I am for the church and unity within the body of Christ. I am however against wrong religious teachings that are misleading. I am asking you to question the things that are being taught these days for your own benefit.

Although there are a lot of people who mean well and have good intentions we need to be aware that there are some teachings out there that we need to be questioning instead of just accepting them as truth. I have learned from the Holy Spirit that it is never a good idea to point an accusing finger at someone and say you are wrong, that will only put them on the defensive. Rather it's better to point out the truth according to scripture.

Many people are taking some Old Testament scriptures and turning them into a teaching and trying to apply them to the new covenant of grace. Another misuse of scripture is taking one or two lines of scripture and making a teaching out of it. When you read the Bible you need to keep in mind the times in which they are speaking, the audience they are speaking to and the context.

Regarding the scripture below, Hebrews 10:20, it is talking about the Holy veil that was in the temple and that when Jesus died on the cross He completely destroyed that veil.

Hebrews 10:17-20 And their sins and iniquities will I remember no more. Now where remission of these is, there is no more offering for sin. Having therefore, brethren, boldness to enter into the holiest by the blood of Jesus, By a new and living way, which he hath consecrated for us, through the veil, that is to say, his flesh.

There is a teaching going around that talks about tearing of the veil and says you can step through this veil when you want to be in God's presence and then step back out. Again, the two scriptures below point out that the veil was torn in two by God Himself! It's gone! There is no more veil to step through! I would rather stand believing in faith what the word says that His presence is within me.

Matthew 27:51 And, behold, the veil of the temple was rent in twain from the top to the bottom; and the earth did quake, and the rocks rent.

Luke 23:45 And the sun was darkened, and the veil of the temple was rent in the midst.

Hebrews 13:5…for he hath said, I will never leave thee, nor forsake thee.

Another teaching says that instead of using your authority here on earth like Jesus told us to do you should ascend into some heavenly court room and plead your case to God defending yourself against the accusations that the devil has brought against you. I have even heard that someone took somebody into one of these court rooms in the spirit without them being aware of it. Our authority was not given to us so that we could use it against people it was given to us to be used against demonic spirits that are afflicting people.

Ephesians 6:12 For we wrestle not against flesh and blood, but against principalities, against powers, against the rulers of the darkness of this world, against spiritual wickedness in high places.

If we do anything without someone's consent then that becomes witchcraft! It is the enemy that tries to get people to use their authority to accomplish his will. Satan has no authority. He's been stripped of all power and authority by Jesus. Satan is the one that tries to go against God's will and do things behind someone's back, not God!

I heard someone say that they went into a court room in the second heaven and that there are courts there that are left over from the Old Testament. The second heaven is where all the wicked principalities and rulers of darkness reside; we have no business going there.

Our authority is to be used on this earth only, not in heavenly realms. I cannot find anywhere in scripture were Jesus instructs us to ascend into some heavenly court room. In fact, He told me this whole thing about these court rooms is a cop out. If you understand your authority then there is no reason to ever go there.

The Vine's Bible dictionary gives some examples of how this word court is used throughout scripture. The word court is described as the outer courtyard or grounds of the sanctuary and the temple. It is also translated "village or town". It also refers to the court yard of a prison. Jesus was taken to a municipal court, and so was Paul. They have tried to use scriptures like the ones listed below to say that there is some sort of heavenly court where judgment is now taking place.

Daniel 7:9-10 I beheld till the thrones were cast down, and the Ancient of days did sit, whose garment was white as snow, and the hair of his head like the pure wool: his throne was like the fiery flame, and his wheels as burning fire. A fiery stream issued and came forth from before him: thousand thousands ministered unto him, and ten thousand times ten thousand stood before him: the judgment was set, and the books were opened.

Revelations 20:11-12 And I saw a great white throne, and him that sat on it, from whose face the earth and the heaven fled away; and there was found no place for them. And I saw the dead, small and great, stand before God; and the books were opened: and another book was opened, which is the book of life: and the dead were judged out of those things which were written in the books, according to their works.

These scriptures in both Daniel and the book of Revelation are both talking about the end times, what is to come in the future, where there will be a great time of judgment. Of course this is not happening now as those previously mentioned teachings would somehow suggest.

Jesus told us to go out and preach the gospel because the only way people can be set free is if someone tells them the truth. The devil would like nothing more than for you to lock yourself in your closet and spend all of your time begging and pleading trying to get God to change someone when He has told you to go do it.

Matthew 28:17-20 And when they saw him, they worshipped him: but some doubted. And Jesus came and spake unto them, saying, All power is given unto me in heaven and in earth. Go ye therefore,

*and teach all nations, baptizing them in the name of the Father,
and of the Son, and of the Holy Ghost: Teaching them to observe all
things whatsoever I have commanded you: and, lo, I am with you
alway, even unto the end of the world. Amen.*

There is no need to do spiritual warfare trying to clear some
hole in the atmosphere in order to get your prayer up to God.
His Holy Spirit is in you and He always hears you. If God wants
to answer your prayer by sending an angel then nothing is going
to stop them now like there was in the old testament (Daniel
10:12-13) and there is no such thing as a portal.

Remember Jesus has stripped the entire demonic realm of
all power and authority. Angels behold the face of God and they
listen to Him, not you, we have no business commanding angels;
they are not under our authority. Notice the scriptures below
state that they are <u>His</u> angels, they are waiting for God to give
them instructions and they only listen to <u>His</u> voice and obey <u>His</u>
commands.

*Matthew 18:10 Take heed that ye despise not one of these little ones;
for I say unto you, That in heaven their angels do always behold the
face of my Father which is in heaven.*

*Psalms 103:20 Bless the LORD, ye his angels, that excel in strength,
that do his commandments, hearkening unto the voice of his word.*

*Psalms 91:11 For he shall give his angels charge over thee, to keep
thee in all thy ways.*

I want to see people grow and become more secure in who
they have become in Christ and eventually see that they are

lacking nothing. You really can do all things through Christ who strengthens you. The Holy Spirit has inspired me to point out the things that are holding people back. He wants us to recognize these things that I have shared with you in this book so that you can avoid them. Many people want to experience more of God but they are stuck because of the environment and wrong teachings that they have been exposed to. Church should be making disciples and providing ways in which people can frequently use their supernatural gifting on a regular basis. Part of learning is by doing, we are never going to flow in these gifts if we aren't using them. Just sitting in a church like a knot on a log is not going to produce disciples.

Church should be fun not boring. The general public should be able to go to a church and receive healing whenever they need it and not have to wait until the church decides that maybe one of these days we will have a healing service.

IT'S TIME FOR A CHANGE

The modern day American church is broken and it needs to be fixed. The only way that this is going to happen is if we all work together. We first need to know the truth because it's knowing the truth that will set us free from all this religious bondage. Once we are free then we can begin to help others overcome the things that are holding them back. We could start making disciples out of people by simply sharing the truth with them even if it's only one person at a time. We are all going to have work at this because if we are ever going to see this country turn around, that influence is going to have to come from the church, we can't expect that the government will turn things around on their own. The church needs to demonstrate that they are able to walk in power and authority before anyone is going to listen to them.

There needs to be a great awaking in the church in America. We need to know who we are in Christ and recognize the power that has been placed in us before we can effectively demonstrate any kind of display of signs and wonders. We need to do more than just pray and ask God to change our nation. We need to pray and ask God what we can do to help change our nation and then go do it.

> *1 Corinthians 2:4-5 And my speech and my preaching was not with enticing words of man's wisdom, but in demonstration of the Spirit and of power: That your faith should not stand in the wisdom of men, but in the power of God.*
>
> *1 Thessalonians 1:5 For our gospel came not unto you in word only, but also in power, and in the Holy Ghost...*

MY PRAYER FOR YOU

I thank you Father and I pray for everyone that reads this book, that the eyes of their understanding be opened so that they may know that they are completely changed, that their spirit is now a new creation and that now they are one with you forever through Jesus. Father I pray that your Word will give them a revelation of all your fullness that is now in them, and how much you love them and that they will know you will never leave them, in Jesus name. Amen!

Chris and Susan Leffler are founders of Finished Works Ministries. You may contact them via e-mail at: **finishedworksministry@ hotmail.com**.

Susan Leffler is also author and illustrator of the Gracie children's books series.
"The Love of Grace"
"Hearing His Voice with Grace"
"His Word Came by Grace"
"God's Goodness, Gifts and Grace" and "The Beauty and Peace in Grace"

For more information on our founding fathers, the Constitution and how the Bible was used in the formation of our government, go to the website **www.wallbuilders.com**.

www.ingramcontent.com/pod-product-compliance
Lightning Source LLC
LaVergne TN
LVHW091308080426
835510LV00007B/420